First Edition

CAREER COMPASS

Your Ultimate Guide to a Fulfilling Career

By

Mohamed Ibrahim

CAREER COMPASS
ISBN-13: 978-1492284895
ISBN-10: 1492284890
Copyright © Mohamed Ibrahim, 2013
All Rights Reserved

Dedication

To my sweet children Rawan and Ali, for their love that continues to inspire me.

Contents

Preface

"Career Compass" is an integral career management guide for mid and early-career professionals, fresh graduates, and college students. Just like a compass in the hand of an explorer, this book will help you know what your "true north", ideal career is, and will then guide you to pursue it.

With no fluffing or too many buzzwords, this book offers you a step-by-step, hands-on approach to plan, develop, and lead a fulfilling career. The starting point is to assist you -via a complete self-assessment battery- to become aware of your interests, motivators, and strengths. Once you gain this valuable awareness about yourself, you will be shown how to craft a solid career plan that best matches you. After that, the book will illustrate how to work this plan out by offering practical recipes for handling every major step in your journey.

This book strives to strike a balance between the need to grasp the big picture, and the need to nail down the nitty gritty details. While it gives you a strategic mindset on how to think about your professional life and career choices, it also advises you on matters like how to negotiate your salary, how to manage your boss, and how to impress other people, and it goes further down to discuss things like the best font type for your resume and the best suit colour for your job interview.

Acknowledgements

After Allah, I owe my deepest gratitude to my mother, for her unwavering emotional support and encouragement. Without her dedication to maintain a comforting environment for me, this book was not to be completed.

I must also acknowledge Prof. Dr. Mohamed El-Hinnawy, Dean of ESLSCA Business School for his valuable insights that inspired me with lots of ideas for the book, and for his generosity introducing me to a broad professional and academic network that granted me access to a wealth of experiences and case studies.

I cannot forget to be grateful to Robert Terpstra and Fatima El-Saadani, the managing editors of Business Today Egypt, who guided me in my first steps as a business author. Finally, my special thanks are the least I can give to Khaled Fahmy and Dr. Ahmed Amr for their thoughtful comments in reviewing the book.

About The Author

Mohamed Ibrahim is a university lecturer and a management consultant with more than sixteen years of professional experience in strategic planning, program management, and learning and development. He worked in various multinational organizations in Egypt and in the Gulf region.

He currently lives and works in Cairo, Egypt, where he earned his doctorate degree in business administration from the Arab Academy Graduate School of Business (AAGSB). He is also certified as a Six Sigma Black Belt and as a Project Management Professional. He lectures a series of management and leadership courses at ESLSCA Business School.

Dr. Mohamed tries to employ his expertise and knowledge to help people advance their careers, and help organizations get the most out of their people, by offering one-on-one career mentoring as well as tailored training courses in the self-help area, including topics like decision making, interpersonal skills, negotiation, and personal development.

Chapter 1: Know Yourself... Intimately

Some years ago, the following interview was broadcast on an Open University sociology TV programme. An interviewer was talking to a female production-line worker in a biscuit factory. The dialogue went like this:

Interviewer: How long have you worked here?
Production Lady: Since I left school, probably about 15 years.
Interviewer: What do you do?
Production Lady: I take packets of biscuits off the conveyor belt and put them into cardboard boxes.
Interviewer: Have you always done the same job?
Production Lady: Yes.
Interviewer: Do you enjoy it?
Production Lady: Oooh Yes, it's great, everyone is so nice and friendly, and we have a good laugh.
Interviewer (with a hint of disbelief): Really? Don't you find it a bit boring?
Production Lady: Oh no, sometimes they change the biscuits...

This one-minute, true story tells us that the interviewer had a flawed assumption that career fulfillment has the same meaning for everybody, and that all people get motivated at work by the very same things. To the interviewer's surprise, the female production worker seemed fairly satisfied with what he only perceived as a dull job. Perhaps the interviewer believed that a successful career should offer things like intricate tasks, authority, or status, but as for the production worker, it was apparently enough to have a stable job with friendly coworkers.

So, to pursue a career that is most fulfilling to you, you must first have clear answers to these three basic questions: What is the kind of activities that you love to do most? What are the aspects of a job that makes you motivated? And, what is the sort of tasks that you can do best? In light of your answers, search for a career that aligns with your natural preferences and strengths. In brief, to actually "find yourself" in a career, you must first "know yourself" intimately. It all starts here!

To help you attain this necessary knowledge about yourself, this book is equipped with a self-assessment battery in appendix (A). The battery contains ten questionnaire instruments that you can easily fill and interpret, and that measure your interests, motivators, skills, and personality type, among other things.

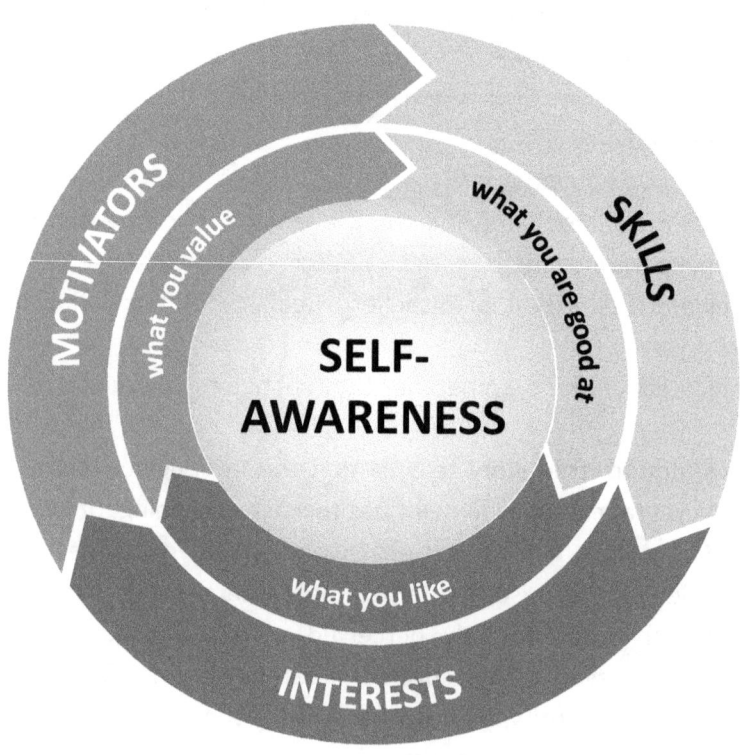

Figure 1.1   Elements of Self-Awareness

1. Explore your interests

It costs you more to do things you are less interested in. Even if you have the skills needed to do these things, you still have to expend more energy to use those skills to mastery. This is a principle called "The Cost of Dis-Interest". To avoid or minimize that cost, you need to explore your interests, and try to align what you do with what you like.

Whether you are just starting out in your career, thinking about a career change, or considering education options for career preparation, you can gain valuable insights about your interests by taking the mini-assessment: What Are My Career Interests? (Pg. 122)

This instrument measures your interests, not your skills or abilities. It assesses your level of interest in each of the below six broad categories of work:

- **Realistic (R)**: Enjoy work activities that include practical, hands-on problems and solutions. They like dealing with plants, animals, and real-world materials, like wood, tools, and machinery. They enjoy outside work.

- **Investigative (I)**: Enjoy work that involves solving complex problems. They like exploring ideas, conducting research and looking at theories. They prefer thinking over doing and prefer data and ideas to people.

- **Artistic (A)**: Enjoy work activities that deal with the artistic side of things, such as forms, designs, and patterns. They like self-expression in their work. They prefer settings where work can be done without following a clear set of rules.

- **Social (S)**: Enjoy work activities that assist others and promote learning and personal development. They prefer to be with people rather than to work with objects, machines, or data. They like to teach, to give advice, to help, or otherwise be of service to people.

- **Enterprising (E)**: Enjoy work activities that have to do with starting up and carrying out projects, especially business ventures. They like persuading and leading people and making decisions. They like taking risks for profit. These people prefer action rather than thought.

- **Conventional (C)**: Enjoy work activities that follow set procedures and routines. They prefer working with data and detail more than with ideas. They prefer work in which there are precise standards rather than make judgments. These people like working where the lines of authority are clear.

The instrument then provides you with a wide variety of career and educational options that match your top interests. Don't expect that all of the options will be equally attractive to you. While interests play a key role in identifying preferred occupations, other factor such as abilities, skills, values, previous experience, and personality type (Pg. 140) also influence what you find appealing. Of course, some of the jobs suggested will match your desires to a greater extent than others.

As you review your results, note your top interest areas and your areas of least interest, and think about how they relate to your work, educational, and leisure activities. Take the time to consider any top interest areas that are not currently part of your work or lifestyle and think about how you might be able to incorporate them into your plans.

2. Understand your motivators

One day, I got a phone call from one of my mentees. She was a young, hard-working, and ambitious professional, but she was perplexed when two exciting career opportunities knocked her door almost at the same time. One opportunity would grant her high visibility through constant exposure to upper levels of management and main decision makers in her organization, while the other one would allow her to foster her creativity and develop her problem solving skills by leading an effort to enhance complex cross-departmental processes. She was asking me: "What would you choose if you were in my shoes?"

I responded to her: "Nobody can choose for you. You must choose for yourself."

And I added: "But, let me tell you my version of the author James Patterson's metaphor: Imagine work is a game in which you are juggling five balls. The balls are called power, autonomy, expertise, creativity, and stability. And you are trying to keep all of them in the air. But one day you finally come to realize that some balls are made of rubber. If you drop them, they will bounce back. The other balls are made of glass. If you drop one of these, it will be irrevocably scuffed, nicked, perhaps even shattered... Now you are the only one who can tell which balls in your game are glass balls and which ones are rubber."

It is important for you too, to know the "glass ball" motivators and the "rubber ball" motivators in your game. This will help you make better career decisions. You can understand and prioritize your own motivators by taking the mini-assessment: What Motivates Me At Work? (Pg. 128)

However, we cannot fully know what our career motivators are until we have had some real work experience. With each new experience we should come closer to understanding what things we really desire more than others. From early on in life many of us know what we want. However, experience will often temper these aspirations and perhaps provide us with new ambitions. There are eight career motivators, for which we all have prioritized preferences:

- **Technical/functional competence**: excited by the content of the work itself, and prefers advancement only in his/her technical or functional specialty.

- **General management competence**: likes harnessing people together to achieve common goals, and is stimulated by crisis situations.

- **Autonomy/independence**: motivated to seek work situations that are free from close supervision, and wants to set own schedule and pace of work.

- **Security/stability**: motivated by job security and long-term attachment to one organization, and tends to dislike travel and relocation.

- **Entrepreneurial creativity**: motivated by the need to build or create something that is entirely their own project.

- **Service/dedication to a cause**: motivated to improve the world in some fashion, and wants to align work activities with personal values about helping society.

- **Pure challenge**: motivated to overcome major obstacles, solve almost unsolvable problems, or win out over extremely tough opponents.

- **Lifestyle**: motivated to balance career with lifestyle, and is highly concerned with such issues as paternity/maternity leave, day care options etc.

3. Know your skills

Skills are things you can do well. They are what you learn and become more adept at doing through practice. Skills become strengths when you can both do things exceedingly well and do them easily without draining you. To have a particular strength, it implies that you must first have an innate talent and then you develop it through learning and practice. Your strengths are your greatest asset. It is rational then to look for a career that plays to your strengths, rather than one that exposes your weaknesses.

The notion that "you can be anything you want to be, if you just try hard enough" is very inspirational, yet mythical. In his book "Strengths Finder", Tom Rath calls it the "Misguided Maxim" that could lead you to waste time, energy, and opportunities in a wrong direction. You will not learn and grow the most in your areas of weakness. Instead you will learn and grow the least in these areas. For instance, if you are not naturally empathetic enough, you can hardly become a star in a customer service role, no matter how much training and practice you do. Similarly, if you have always struggled with numbers, it is unlikely that you will become a great accountant or statistician, no matter how hard you try.

Follow the path of least resistance, not the path of most resistance for you. Know your natural abilities, nurture them with training, practice, and discipline, and pursue a career that capitalizes most on them. It is only then that you could become super at what you do. To know your skills and strengths, take the mini-assessment: What Are My Skills? (Pg. 135)

That instrument allows you to identify the skills you possess in six broad areas that cover a very wide array of professions:

- Basic skills: that facilitate learning or the more rapid acquisition of knowledge

- Complex problem solving skills: used to solve novel, ill-defined problems in complex, real-world settings

- Resource management skills: used to allocate different types of resources efficiently

- Social skills: used to work with people to achieve goals

- Systems skills: used to understand, monitor, and improve socio-technical systems

- Technical skills: used to design, set-up, operate, and maintain machines or technological systems

4. Validate your findings

After completing the three self-assessments mentioned above, write down your top three interests, motivators, and skills in: My Career Profile (Pg. 172) section of the Career Plan Template in appendix (B). Take the time to discuss the results with people who are important to you such as your family, close friends, and career mentors. Ask them about how they see you and how they describe you, and use their feedback to confirm or recheck your findings.

5. Find a career mentor

A career mentor is a professional with great experience, knowledge, or wisdom who will be willing to guide, advise, and encourage you on career-related matters and even personal issues. True mentoring is not just about answering occasional questions or providing ad hoc help. It is about an ongoing relationship of learning, dialogue, and challenge. Even if you are currently working in an organization that doesn't offer formal mentoring programs to its employees, you still have to find your mentor either inside or outside your workplace.

A "mentorship" or a mentoring relationship should be rewarding to both sides. For you, or the "mentee", the rewards can be better career decisions, faster professional development, improved job performance, or support and affirmation from someone you emulate. For the mentor, the reward can be the feeling of more self-actualization for serving others.

When you seek to forge a mentoring relationship, you must make sure that the mentor's background is relevant to your career pursuit. Have a clear agenda, or in other words, ask for the mentor's help on a particular matter, and be sure that the mentor understands what you expect in terms of advice and support. Respect the mentor's time. Follow up, and ask to meet on an ongoing basis.

To get the most out of this mentorship, you must be proactive, open minded and willing to change. Listen to your mentor attentively, act on advice, show commitment to learn, and don't forget to check your ego at the door.

6. Prepare for your journey

The self-awareness you should have obtained by completing this chapter represents the "compass" that will help you find your "True north" career. The career plan you are going to devise over the next chapter will be the "map" that will guide you through your career journey. Chapters 3 to 15 will show you the tools and supplies you need to take with you on that journey. You must have the three things: the compass, the map, and the tools and supplies, to lead a fulfilling career.

Chapter 2: Craft A Solid Career Plan

Did you know that..

Soichiro Honda, the founder of Honda Motor Company was turned down by Toyota Motor Corporation after an interview for an engineering job?

And that Colonel Sanders of Kentucky Fried Chicken had his famous secret chicken recipe rejected 1,009 times before a restaurant accepted it?

And that Walt Disney was fired by a newspaper editor because he was perceived as lacking imagination and good ideas?

And that Winston Churchill was defeated in every election for public office until he finally became the Prime Minister at the age of 62?

And that Julie Andrews was told that she was not photogenic enough for filming after a screen test she took at the age of 12 at MGM Studios?

I'm sure you see the point I'm trying to get across here. There are countless examples of extraordinarily successful people in all fields of life, who were defeated or rejected, but never quit on their dreams. In common between all of these people is something that lent them the determination to overcome life setbacks; something that gave them the unshakeable belief in their ability to turn their dreams into reality, and be who they ought to be. This "something" is simply that each one of them had envisioned where his or her "True North" career is, and then acted to pursue it.

Now is your turn to envision your "True North" career and craft a solid plan to pursue it, in light of the valuable knowledge you have already acquired about your own interests, motivators, and skills. Here are the steps you need to put your career plan:

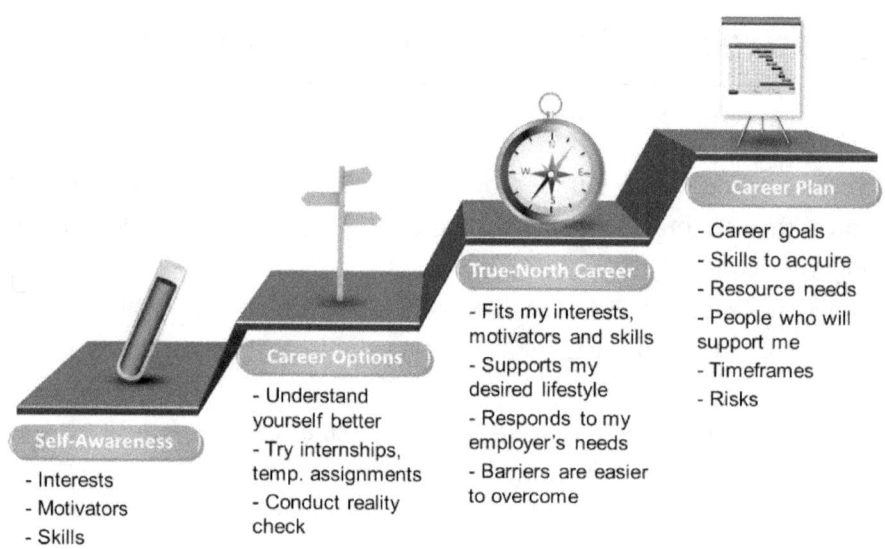

Figure 2.1   Steps of Creating a Career Plan

1. Understand the difference between a career and a job

A career is not a job. A career is a life-time journey of work, learning, and growth. Even if you ponder the Latin origin of the word, which is "cararia", and it means (track for wheeled vehicles), you will arrive at the same meaning. From another perspective, you can think of a career as a sequence of related jobs usually pursued within a given industry or specialty. For example, a career in advertising may include jobs like advertising copywriter, advertising specialist, advertising manager, advertising director, and so on.

So, finding a career is different from and broader than finding a job, in both its goals and its means. This distinction is essential to understanding the nature of career planning. Career planning typically spans several years into the future, and tries to portray what the person will want to be, learn, and do. It also aligns the person's career choices with his or her strengths and preferences.

2. Explore your career options

Whether you are preparing to start your career, or are reevaluating your choices whilst in the middle of your journey, take some time to distance yourself from your daily life hassles, and try to visualize your future. Dream about the brightest possible career you might have, where you will be doing the kind of things you enjoy the most.

Perhaps you didn't yet figure out what your ideal career is, and perhaps you need first to compare between few options before you really "find" yourself in one of them. At that point you should build on the valuable self-awareness you have developed through the first chapter. Without leaving your desk, you can learn about the different career options that best suit your preferences and strengths. Visit O*NET OnLine on: www.onetonline.org, which is the largest occupational information network, and that contains a database of the profiles of more than 970 occupations. Search for occupations that have interest, motivator, and skill profiles similar to yours. You can then identify the different knowledge areas that are prerequisites or mandatory requirements for each of these occupations.

From another side, taking things like internships, temporary assignments, or part-time work can offer you a great opportunity to complement your understanding about your own self and to realistically preview different career fields without risky commitments. After all, you need to refine your career options, and narrow them down to 2-3 options. This will make it easier for you to evaluate and choose between them. Write down your career options along with any comments on their prerequisites, requirements, obstacles, etc. in the section: My Career Options (Pg. 173) of the career plan template.

- **Example**: Laila is a senior student in the faculty of arts. She can't wait to take the first step in her practical life. She dreamed one day of becoming a teacher, emulating one of her secondary school teachers who used to fascinate the whole class with his charisma, deep knowledge, and discipline. Laila, however loves to change scenes frequently and to visit new places. A lifestyle that can go with a job like a tour guide rather than a job of a teacher. In the midst of her indecision whether to pursue a career in education or a career in tourism, Laila received a tempting offer from her uncle to join him after graduation as a sales agent in the auto dealership he is going to launch within few months. Now Laila has three career options to choose from.

First thing Laila did was to take various self-assessments to get a clearer idea about her own interests, motivators, and skills. She then learned from O*NET OnLine database that the closest job to her own profile was the tour guide job, since Laila's top interests were "Social" and "Enterprising", and her top motivators were "Autonomy" and "Service", which closely matched those of a tour guide. The second best match was the sales agent job, and then surprisingly at last was the teacher job.

Laila was still not fully confident about her findings, and so she decided to sign up as a teaching intern in a summer school program. Despite the initial joy she felt while tutoring students, she quickly got bored because of the enormous amount of record filling, material preparation and paperwork she had to finish every week. That internship gave Laila the chance to confirm the results of her self-assessments and to more practically evaluate her career options.

Finally, and also through O*NET OnLine database, Laila was able to identify the prerequisites or requirements needed to pursue each career option. The tour guide job would require Laila to take some studies like a history diploma. The sales agent job would demand her to get trainings on persuasion and negotiation skills, and the teacher job would mandate that she obtains some knowledge in psychology and learning strategies.

3. Perform reality check

While you have your head in the clouds, trying to picture the ideal career you dream about, you must have your feet on the ground. You must know whether the career choices you are considering will allow you to earn the amount of money needed to pay your bills and support your desired lifestyle. Think about the city you'd want to live in, the people you'd like to meet, the house you'd dream to own, the car you'd love to drive, the hobbies you'd enjoy to pursue, the health care you'd wish to secure, and so on. Think about all of these things, and check if the income you expect to earn from your chosen career can afford them.

One very useful starting point that can help you obtain a reliable and updated estimate of the average pay you are going to get is the website: www.salaryexpert.com. It offers access to salary information for over 100,000 job titles in 69 countries. You must also talk to friends and recruiters, and perhaps attend some job interviews before you can have a more concrete idea about the salary range that you may expect to earn. Record whether each of your career options can support your desired lifestyle in the section: My Career Options (Pg. 173) of the career plan template.

- **Example**: Continuing the case of Laila, after she conducted the reality check for the three career options, she found that they all can allow her to earn an annual salary of around $23,000. She estimated the cost of living in her city and found that it could be reasonably supported by such income. Due to similarity of the income levels granted by all career options, it will not be a significant factor in choosing between them. After exploring her career options and conducting the necessary reality checks, Laila documented all information in the career options section of her career plan. It will look like the following figure:

MY CAREER OPTIONS			
		Comments (e.g., prerequisites, requirements, obstacles, etc.)	Desired Lifestyle Supported? (Y/N)
Option 1:	Tour Guide	Knowledge about history	Y
		Foreign languages	
Option 2:	Sales Agent	Knowledge about sales and marketing	Y
		Knowledge about mathematics	
		Persuasion & negotiation skills	
Option 3:	Teacher	Knowledge about psychology	Y
		Knowledge about learning strategies	
		Administrative and paperwork burden	

Figure 2.2   Example of Career Options Section in a Career Plan

4. Choose your "True North" career

After identifying and exploring your career options along with their prerequisites, requirements, and obstacles, and after performing the reality checks, you should be now more ready to envision your "True North" career. Answering the below questions honestly will help you settle the needle of your compass and decide on the best career option to pursue:

- Which career option best fits my interests, skills, and motivators?

- Which career option best supports my desired lifestyle?

- What are the barriers/obstacles facing each career option and how can they be overcome?

- To what extent is my current role aligned with my interests, skills, and motivators (if you are already employed)?

- Which career option responds best to the needs of my current employer (if you are already employed)?

16

Write down your "True North" career in the section: <u>My True North Career</u> (Pg. 174) of the career plan template. This is the best career choice for you, given the many factors we have discussed.

- **Example**: Back to Laila, in light of her possible answers to the above questions, and considering the ranking of her three career options, she would choose a career as a tour guide. This is her "True North" career.

5. Set your career goals

Your career goals represent the new roles you plan to assume and all the moves you intend to make, that will support your career choice. It is advisable that your plan caters for short-range goals covering one year or less, medium-range goals, covering two years, and long-range goals, covering three to five years in the future. It is needless to say that just like any other goals you may set (e.g., life goals, study goals, or professional goals), your career goals must be SMART, meaning they must be **S**pecific (Quantifiable), **M**easureable (can be measured to know if they are achieved or not), **A**chievable (difficult but not impossible to attain, so that they are motivating to pursue), **R**elevant (meaningful and supporting to your career choice), and **T**ime-bounded (to be achieved within a certain time frame).

You also need to assess your current skills and knowledge areas, and check if you need to upgrade any of them or develop new ones, to be able to attain your career goals. This might be done through many ways like: taking work assignments in other areas of business, shadowing people in upper management levels, seeking lateral moves, attending classroom training or on-the-job training, continuing one's education, registering for professional certifications, signing up for internships, or joining volunteering work.

A realistic plan must not omit the resources you will need and the people who will help you to reach your career goals. Resources can be things like money, staff, properties, or equipment. People include powerful persons who can shape events and create or assign opportunities, social hubs who will grant you access to big professional networks, advisors who will share with you valuable insights about your field or industry, and family members and friends who will give you the needed emotional support. In the section: My Career Goals (Pg. 174) of the career plan template, write down:

- Your career goals

- The reasons these goals are important to your career choice

- Skills you will need to acquire

- Resources that are needed

- People who will support you

- Implementation timeframes.

- **Example**: After Asking friends, family, local travel agencies, teachers and career counselors, and after reading about the travel industry in the media and websites, Laila was able to chart a clearer path for herself. The career goals section of her plan will look like the following figure:

MY CAREER GOALS							
	Goal	How Does It Support My Career Choice?	Skills I Must Acquire To Reach That Goal	How Will I Acquire These Skills?	Resources I Need (Money, Staff, etc.)	People Who Will Support Me	Time Frame
Short-range (1 Year)	Join tourism industry in any role in tour operations	Get exposure needed to move to a tour guiding career	- Service orientation	- Work as temp. sales agent in uncle's dealership	None	- My uncle - Friends in local travel agencies	Fourth quarter, 2013
Mid-range (2 Years)	Assume a tour guide role in a nationwide travel agency	Enjoy serving others and achieve the lifestyle I want	- Knowledge about history - Foreign languages	- History diploma - Spanish & Italian courses	- Diploma fees ($400) - Course fees ($300)	- Join main travel industry associations in the country	First half, 2015
Long-range (3-5 Years)	Advance to a tour manager or operations manager role	Grow and fulfill my future aspirations	- Supervisory skills - Administration skills	- Work experience - Trainings & Business studies	- Company educational support	- Network with key people in the organization	2017-2018

Figure 2.3   Example of Career Goals Section in a Career Plan

6. Put a contingency plan

Life is what happens to you while you are busy making other plans. Or, is it not? Even the most well-thought-out plans may fail in responding to life uncertainties. In one example I saw, a middle manager crafted a rosy plan with ambitious career progression goals, to find out after a year or so that his company began to undertake a drastic cost reduction program in which it would lay off hundreds of jobs including possibly his own job. In another case, a specialist was planning to enroll for an advanced educational program, only to learn one month prior to the commencement date that the program's prerequisites have been made much tougher, so that she is not qualified for that program anymore.

So, you must put some flexibility into your plan by accounting for the major risks that could hamper its implementation. Try to gather enough information and anticipate the various risks that may impact your career goals. Rank all risks based on the rating (High, Medium, and Low) that you assign to each of them. This rating should reflect both the likelihood and the severity of the risk. Focus mainly on your top three to five risks and put in place some counteracting measures against each. These measures must try to eliminate the risk or at least mitigate its impact should it occurs. Write down the major risks you anticipate and the measures that will help you counteract their impact in the section: My Career Risk Management Plan (Pg. 175) of the career plan template.

- **Example**: After giving a second thought about her career goals and what it takes to achieve them, and after some discussions with her family, Laila was able to anticipate two important risks. First, there could be some delay in her uncle's plan to launch his dealership. This implies that she must start looking for an alternative temp job (preferably in the tourism sector itself) to help her acquire the needed skill of service orientation, and to secure the money necessary to pay the fees of the education and training programs she plans to join. Second, Laila came to know that her elder sister is planning to return from her expat assignment within a year or so, where she will need Laila's assistance in settling back. This means that Laila has to accelerate some of her education or training plans, so that she could have the time to help her sister when she is back. Now the risk management section of Laila's career plan will look like the following figure:

MY CAREER RISK MANAGEMENT PLAN			
Risk	**Risk Rating (H/M/L)**	**Career Goals Impacted**	**Counteracting Measures**
Delay in launching uncle's auto dealership	M	Join tourism industry (I will not be able to acquire the Skill of service orientation)	Search for alternative temp Jobs
More time needed to my help sister settle back	M	Assume a tour guide role (I will not be able to timely gain the needed knowledge)	Accelerate my foreign Language training programs

Figure 2.4   Example of Risk Management Section in a Career Plan

7. Select your job search strategy

Do you know that searching for a job is considered one of our life's primary causes of stress, ranking just up there beside events like divorce and the loss of a loved one? The rules of the game are even getting harder with the gloomy worldwide economic outlook and the more than ever furious competition for every role. So, you need to adopt a job search strategy that maximizes your chances landing the job you aspire for.

There are numerous sources of information that can help you on your job search: job ads in the press, government agencies (e.g. your local Job Centre), private employment agencies, professional journals, phone book company listings, internet search engines, company websites, social media, people you know (e.g., friends, colleagues, former employers and teachers), job clubs, career fairs, and volunteering work.

The advice here is to rely on active methods more than passive methods. It's very tempting to lull into the easy passive methods like uploading your resume to a recruitment website, and waiting for things to happen. But does this often pay off? Use your connections first. Ask people you know who might know of vacancies that suit you, and ask your former bosses, teachers, and work colleagues for recommendations. I'm personally amazed to find out that two thirds of the jobs I got across my career so far were through my own professional network. Your professional network is your second greatest asset, just after your skills and abilities.

In parallel to asking people in your professional network, you may also need to knock on the doors of companies you wish to work for. Get the names and contact data of prospective employers and their representatives, and call them first. Never send your resume unannounced. Always make the phone your primary tool for contacting potential employers.

If your dream job is not showing itself quickly enough, then you might take the advice of Sue Greener and her coauthors in their book: "Graduate Employment", and consider a range of possibilities including: working part-time, taking temp project work, consultancy, telework, on-call, or job-share. Such flexible work arrangements may not be the conventional way to start a graduate career, yet they can help you build a richer portfolio of work experiences, and allow you more freedom to organize your time.

8. Tips for your first job:

Your first job is the first rung in your career ladder. Here are a few tips on that can help you on your first job:

- Start out in a big organization and department that is high in power. This will grant you wider exposure and will facilitate your next move.

- Do good work. That's a necessary but not sufficient condition for success.

- Project the right image by aligning your behaviors with what the organization values.

- Develop your Knowledge and expertise so that you become more valuable. Employees who embrace life-long learning can add value and are needed by today's organizations.

- Stay visible. Provide progress reports, participate in cross-departmental assignments, be active in professional associations, and develop powerful allies.

- Stay mobile. You may need to change geographical locations, or move across functional boundaries.

- Think laterally. Consider lateral career moves to widen your experiences, and increase your long-term mobility.

- Support your boss, and if your boss is not competent, you may need to move to another job.

- Learn the power structure. Both formal and informal relationships are important.

- Develop a network. Friends, colleagues, neighbors, customers, suppliers, etc. can help you get things done and find a new job when you need one.

- Don't stay too long in your first job.

Chapter 3: Write A Resume That Makes Your Phone Rings

Your resume is the main document that makes you noticeable to and searchable by potential employers. The function of a resume is not to land you a job, but just to make employers interested enough to call you for an interview. But you know that recruiters receive tens or maybe hundreds of resumes for any particular job posting, so chances are that they spend only a minute or so skimming through each. Only a tiny fraction of resumes recruiters receive, survive this initial screening (filtering) and stir enough attention of the recruiter to take a couple of more minutes and read them thoroughly, let alone calling the applicant for an interview.

Over this chapter, I will be sharing with you the secrets to writing a resume that will let you stand out of the crowd, and make recruiters pick up the phone to call you for a job interview. I will try here to answer questions like: What are the contents of a resume? Do you need a resume or a Curriculum Vitae? What is the most suitable resume layout for you? What is the optimum formatting and length of a resume? And what are the most common resume mistakes to avoid?

Resume Writing Secrets:

- A Resume Or A CV?
- Personal Brand Statement
- Chronological Or Functional Layout?
- Formatting And Length
- Common Mistakes To Avoid

Figure 3.1   Resume Writing Secrets

1. What are the contents of a resume?

When a recruiter or a hiring manager checks a candidate's resume, they are looking for answers to two basic questions: Who are you? (i.e. what are your experience, achievements, education, and skills?), and Why should we hire you? (i.e. How are you going to utilize your specific strengths to fill the need/gap that we have?). An effective resume needs to offer answers to these questions. So, your resume must include:

- **Personal information**: your name and your contact details (address, phone number: home/cell/work, email address, and URLs for your social media pages). The best placement of your name is on the title of the first page of your resume, and the best placement of the contact details is on the header of the same page.

- **Career objective**: is a brief statement describing the position you are applying for. It should quickly tell employers which type of role (industry, business area and working level) they should consider you for. An example of a career objective statement is: *"Seeking a challenging middle management role in sales with an admirable employer in the real estate sector, with a room for upward advancement based on performance"*.

More recently, career objective statement is being replaced by a "personal brand" statement. While the career objective statement focuses more on the job you are applying for, the personal brand statement focuses more on "you". It is a statement that describes your personal contribution or added value you are going to offer the employer. In other words it is a means of marketing and differentiating yourself from other applicants (competitors), as if you are a unique brand. An example of a personal brand statement is: *"Relentless and passionate sales manager, who capitalizes on his high commercial acumen to build compelling proposals and conclude sales deals that will help your company achieve its ambitious growth targets, while developing and coaching highly performing sales teams"*.

- **Work experience**: your work experience is one of the most important sections of a resume. It outlines your employment history including positions you've held, responsibilities you've assumed, and accomplishments you've realized at previous employers. They need to be listed in a reverse chronological order starting from your latest position, and backwards.

Many employers want to see your specific (quantifiable) achievements and the meaning (significance or impact) of these achievements, rather than a mere description of your day-to-day routine duties. The reason for this is that they want to know how valuable you were as a contributor to the success of organizations you worked for, and they use this to judge your potential to perform well in future roles.

An example of a specific and meaningful achievement for an office manager could be: *"Reduced the time required to prepare incident reports by 25% over the year 2012, by eliminating redundant steps in the information collection process, thereby helping management make critical decisions faster"*.

Another example for a logistics manager is: *"Managed to cut inventory ordering costs from 80 pounds per order in 2012 to 60 pounds per order in 2013, as a result of deploying automated warehouse management system, which granted our company a clear cost advantage over its competitors"*.

To make the above achievement statements more meaningful, we didn't just say *"reduced the time by 4 hours"*, or *"cut the cost by 20 pounds"*, since it is not enough for the reader to sense the magnitude of these achievements without having any reference to the base/original performance levels (for instance, if the original report preparation time was 12 working days and the original ordering cost was 800 pounds, then the stated improvements would have been so trivial).

Finally, note also that it's more enticing to use action verbs like *"Reduced"* and *"Managed"*, than using static phrases like *"Responsible for"* or *"In charge of"*.

- **Education**: this section outlines the academic qualifications you possess. They need to be listed in a reverse chronological order starting from the latest degree you've attained, and backwards. The relative importance of this section (and accordingly, its placement in your resume) will depend on some factors:

- If you have five or more years of work experience related to your career goal, place the work experience section before the education section. Hiring managers will be more interested in your job accomplishments than your education.

26

- If you are a fresh graduate or have less than five years of work experience, are changing careers and have continued your education to support your new career goal, or if you are an academic or a scientific professional, then place the education section before the work experience section.

In the latter case, you may use the education section as the centerpiece of your resume, demonstrating your academic achievements, extracurricular activities, special projects and related courses. Include any academic honors (e.g. summa cum laude, magna cum laude) to show you excelled in your program. List your GPA if it is 3.0 or higher. Consider including a lower GPA only if you are in a very challenging program. Add your major GPA if it's higher than your overall GPA. As your career progresses, college GPA becomes less important and can be removed.

If you abandoned a college educational program, list the number of credit hours completed or the type of study undertaken. If you don't have a degree but have been participating in an ongoing training, list your related courses, seminars, and conferences under a section called: "Professional Development". Your training might be so impressive to the extent that it compensates for a lack of a formal degree. Include your high school education only if you don't have any college credits. If you have college credits, remove references to high school.

- **Skills**: this section outlines the various skills you've obtained either through education or previous job experience. It can help employers understand the strengths you bring to the table. Examples of skills one could include are computer program proficiencies, administrative skills, and foreign languages.

- **Interests**: this section includes any considerable involvement in extracurricular activities, like high level of achievement (championships, prizes, or awards) in sports, games, societies, or hobbies. The value of this information is that it can tell employers something about your commitment and drive to achieve. Generally you should only include items that you feel will help employers understand your strengths better, rather than including something just for the sake of having it.

2. Do you need a resume or Curriculum Vitae?

If you are a senior executive, lawyer, professor, physician or a scientist, then you will likely need to write a Curriculum Vitae (CV) instead of resume. A CV, in comparison to a resume, is a much longer document (5 to 10 pages) that is highly detailed. Beyond the standard contents of a resume, a CV includes a range of sections like:

- Professional licenses or certifications.
- Listing of relevant course work to match career or academic objective.
- Scientific or academic research, laboratory experience, grants received.
- Description of thesis or dissertation (if you have advanced degrees).
- Papers, books and other related publications you have written.
- Academic or professional presentations and speaking engagements.
- Travel/exposure to cultural experiences.
- Related extracurricular activities, professional and association memberships.
- Letters of recommendation or a list of references.
- Professional development you have undertaken.

Some employers are very specific about what they want to see and how the information should be laid out in a CV. Make sure you read any instructions provided by employers in their job postings, and customize your CV accordingly.

3. What is the most suitable resume layout for you?

There are basically two resume layouts: the chronological resume and the functional resume. The chronological resume is the most popular layout. It contains a chronological listing (from most recent to past) of all your positions along with related accomplishments. This type of resume suits those who have work solid experience relevant to the jobs they are applying for.

Functional resumes highlight your competencies (such as leading others, strategic planning, contract negotiations, etc.), rather than your chronological work history. You'll still need to summarize your work history, but this is usually done at the bottom of the work experience section. A functional resume is particularly useful for those who:

- Have gaps in their work history or are reentering the workforce.
- Have frequently changed jobs.
- Are looking to transition into new careers.

The reason functional resumes work well in these situations is that many of us have acquired skills while working, that are very transferable (refer to chapter 12 for more on the idea of transferable knowledge). For example, if you have worked as a retail manager, chances are that you were responsible for hiring, training, coaching, evaluating and handling employee relations issues; skills that you will most probably reuse if you decide to switch to a career in human resources management. If you were to submit this information in a chronological resume, there's a good chance that a hiring manager might screen you out, because you did not hold the title of human resources manager, even if 50 percent of your day was spent dealing with HR-related issues.

4. What is the optimum formatting and length of a resume?

A winning resume is a game of both content and appearance. Choosing proper and consistent font types, sizes, and styles, and leaving appropriate white space, will make your resume catchy and easily readable. Simple, clean fonts like Arial or Verdana can be suitable. Use a font size of 10.5 to 12 points to obtain excellent readability and to be able to fit a good amount of content into your resume.

Use bold style only for section headers. Don't use italic words or phrases, as scanning systems might have problems reading such characters. You can use all capital letters in headers, but don't write entire sentences in capitals. Stick to one font type and a couple of styles for the whole resume, and apply the Black colour to all the text.

As for the length of your resume, it can range from one page to four pages depending on your experience and on the depth of your technical knowledge you want to prove. There is no hard-and-fast rule that works for every employer, but you must always strive to make your resume concise, and to make sure every word adds value by promoting you to potential employers. Remove redundancies and avoid cramming your resume with information that is irrelevant to your current goal, and ensure you comply with employer requirements (if any) regarding the resume length.

5. What are the most common resume mistakes to avoid?

Perhaps the worst resume mistakes one may ever commit are spelling and grammar mistakes and formatting inconsistencies. They instantly convey the message that you are a reckless person, for if you cannot pay enough attention making such a vital document like your resume free from errors, then where else will you be attentive? To avoid these silly mistakes, it is not enough to proofread your resume by yourself neither by relying entirely on spelling/grammar checkers available with your word processing software. You must get someone else to proofread it. A second eye could greatly help catch these errors.

Another mistake is not incorporating keywords that hiring managers will use to search resume databases. This means that your resume will not show up to them even if you actually are a qualified candidate. To make sure your resume doesn't miss important keywords, study job advertisements since they spell out what hiring managers are looking for, and ask recruiters and employers what credentials are important in your field. Listen to the language hiring managers use to discover keywords you should incorporate in your resume.

Some applicants commit the mistake of writing unnecessary information that might be used by employers to discriminate against them, such as their age, marital status, or personal beliefs. Thus, you need to make sure not to include such information, so as to protect your neutrality on job applications. You don't want to be dismissed from being considered for a job solely based on criteria that have little, or nothing, to do with the role itself.

Chapter 4: Master The Job Interview Process

Good news! Your phone rings and the caller is a potential employer who invites you for an interview. Now what? First you need to understand what job interviews are for. As Tony Beshara, the number one career placement expert in the U.S., says, employers use interviews to answer four basic questions: Can you handle the work? Are you likeable? Do you pose any risk? Can they reach a salary agreement with you?

But, you also need to realize that an interview is a two-way process in which you -as a job seeker- have the opportunity to assess the employer and the position. After reading this chapter, you will be in a far better position to understand the different types of job interviews, prepare yourself for the different interview questions, know what things you should ask about, learn how you should dress for an interview, become aware of the interviewee mistakes you must avoid, and understand how to follow up after an interview.

1. Types of interviews

In essence, there are three types of interviews: the traditional interview, the competency-based interview, and the case interview. The traditional interview includes:

- Background questions that seek to confirm or clarify the information in the candidate's resume, and they focus on work experience, education, and other qualifications (for instance, an interviewer may ask: "What experience have you had with telesales?").

- Technical questions that may ask the candidate to describe or demonstrate specialized knowledge on a particular job aspect (for example, one question may be "What are the components of a feasibility study on a small scale initiative?").

- The brain teaser questions that were popularized by Microsoft in the 1990s, and is now used in many other organizations. They either ask the candidate to solve puzzles or unusual problems (e.g., "How many golf balls can fit in a school bus?"), or request the candidate to estimate the size of a given market (e.g., "What is the number of gas stations in Greater Cairo?").

The competency-based interview is particularly useful when it is hard to solely select on the basis of technical merit. The interviewer attempts to predict how well the candidate will perform in a future role based on her responses to two possible types of questions:

- Behavioral questions which are past-oriented in that they ask respondents to describe situations in their past jobs or lives where they demonstrated a certain behavior or competency that is in fact closely relevant to the future job (e.g., "Give me an example from your previous role where you displayed leadership abilities?").

- Situational questions which are future-oriented in that they ask respondents to imagine a set of circumstances and then indicate how they would respond (e.g., "Imagine that you have a deadline and you are running out of time. What would you do?").

The case interview is an interview form used mostly by management consulting firms and investment banks in which the job applicant is given a business problem or challenge and asked to resolve it. The problem is often a business case that the interviewer has worked on in real life. Resolving such cases may require some knowledge about strategic planning, marketing, or finance.

2. How to prepare for an interview

The first step to prepare for an interview is to do a research and gather as much information as possible about the organization, the position you applied for, and the interviewer. Visit the company's website, check industry reports and business magazines, or call your insider friends to learn about things like:

- History of the organization
- Products or services it offers
- Financial performance of the firm
- Main customers, competitors, and suppliers
- Offices, locations, and number of employees
- Structure/hierarchy of the organization
- Culture and main values of the firm
- Salary range and benefits offered by the firm for the job you applied for
- Progress opportunities
- Skills required to do the job you applied for
- Management style of the hiring manager
- Character of the interviewer

Obtaining such insights is a homework you must do if you want to stand out of the crowd and impress the interviewer by the answers you will give and the questions you will pose. Knowing you will eagerly do this homework, I'll now draw on my own experience and on that of top recruiters to share with you a list of the most frequently asked questions and their ideal answers for every type of interviews:

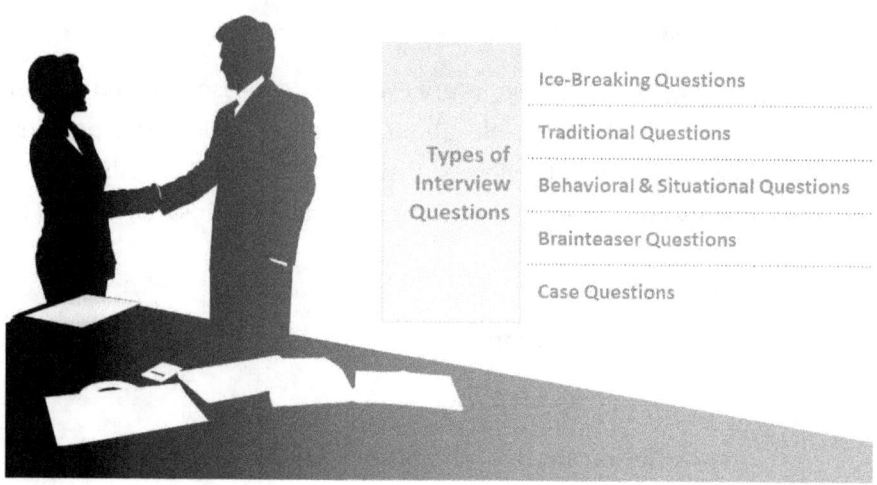

Types of Interview Questions

- Ice-Breaking Questions
- Traditional Questions
- Behavioral & Situational Questions
- Brainteaser Questions
- Case Questions

Figure 4.1   Types of Interview Questions

- Ice-breaking questions: These are broad opening questions asked by the interviewer to make you feel more comfortable in the setting. Make them an opportunity to quickly build rapport with the interviewer and leave a positive impression that sets the tone for the rest of the interview. As Gavin F. Redelman emphasizes in his book "Interview Secrets Exposed", this kind of questions cannot get you the job, but on the other hand it certainly can ruin your chances if answered lamely. Examples of ice-breakers are: "Were there any problem finding our office?", "Would you like some coffee?", or "How do you find that weather?" The best way to answer these questions is to keep your answer related to the question, and be brief, confident and polite.

- Traditional questions: Answer closed ended questions (e.g., yes or no questions) in brief but in one complete sentence not just one word. For instance:

- Are you proficient in using Microsoft Project?
Yes, I'm an advanced MS project user, and I'm also proficient in Primavera.

As for open ended questions, they are the place to elaborate. Plan your answers ahead of the interview, but don't memorize them word for word. Here are the most common questions:

1- Tell me a bit about yourself.
Stay focused on your career and professional accomplishments, particularly those relevant to the job you are applying for. If it could help, you may also refer to any extracurricular activities you are involved in, but remember that the interviewer doesn't wish to hear your personal life story.

2- Why do you want to leave your job?
Never ever talk negatively about your company, boss or colleagues. This will surely backfire on your own image. Don't also mention that it's because your management doesn't like you. State that you like what you do, however, you seek opportunities to grow professionally and you see that this new job is the right career choice for you.

3- What's your greatest strength?
That question is a good chance to show the value you can add. Avoid cliché responses like "I'm loyal" or "I'm a hard worker". Think instead about some of your personal traits or qualities that are demanded by the job you are applying for. For example, if it's a customer service job, it will be quite helpful to mention that your greatest strength is friendliness or patience. If it's a sales job, then it might be your competitiveness or your ability to persuade others that are of great value, and so on. After all, always be honest.

4- What's your biggest weakness?
That's a hard question and you must be careful about your answer. It must be something related to business, not personal life. Saying things like "I'm a lousy cooker" or "I'm terrible at golf" is a bad answer. Cliché responses like "I'm a perfectionist" are just as bad. You must not however say something so dangerous that it could hinder your chances getting the job. If you are applying for a contracts specialist job, you

cannot say your biggest weakness is attention to details. The best way to answer this question is to give a work-related flaw that is not significant to the job you are applying for, and yet to mention that you are already working to improve. As an example, for that same contracts specialist job, you could say: "My presentation skills are not as strong as I'd like, but I signed up for an evening class on presentation skills".

5- Why did you apply for this job?
Use the knowledge you gained about the job and the company to show that you are genuinely motivated to perform on that job and to work for that company. Don't mention money or benefits.

6- Where else did you apply?
Mention a couple of other places. It gives the interviewer the impression that you are serious about your job search. But, mentioning too many places or jobs you've applied for may convey the wrong message that you are desperately trying.

7- You stayed short periods of time in your last three jobs. What's wrong?
This is another tough question. Hold some personal accountability and also try to paint as positive a picture as you can. For example, you might say, "I made some poor career choices in the past. But I have learned from them. After a few false starts, I now know exactly what I want. Your job will be perfect for me. If you hire me, I hope to work for your organization for a long time to come."

8- Were you fired? And, why?
Stay honest, positive, and brief. Don't get emotional. Thousands of people get fired and then get hired again. Turn the negative into positive and let the interviewer know you've learned from that experience. Try also to shift the discussion to previous jobs where you did well and to the good references that you have from those companies.

9- Why should we hire you?

I wouldn't get bored of repeating over and over that you must strive to position yourself uniquely with regard to your competition. Remember how you crafted your personal brand statement in the past chapter, and also check chapter 8: "Impress Others" to see how to hone your "edge". The message they must get clearly is that they should hire you because you are the candidate with the right blend of skills (strengths or talents that will directly benefit the job) and attitude (passion and energy), and this blend positions you to perfectly matches that job requirements, and effortlessly fit within that organization. Realize the fine line between pride in yourself and arrogance, and make sure your body language is reinforcing your spoken words.

In planning your response to that question, take a pen and paper and write down a list of the skills you bring to each major area of responsibility of the job you are applying for. Support this list with examples of your past achievements.

Example response for a product development manager can be: "As you can see, I was able to introduce three of the top successful products to the market over the past couple of years. I built from scratch and led a winning team that consistently achieved a record five months concept-to-launch that beats the industry standard. Shooting star products to the market is the kind of thing I love to do most, and is what I wish to keep doing. So, I bring to the table a wealth of experience and enthusiasm which I believe can help your organization refocus and streamline its product development efforts to remain innovative and competitive."

10- Where do you see yourself in five years time?

One purpose of that question is for the interviewer to know whether you are posing any risks, as they don't really want to hire you, train you and invest in you to see you leaving the firm after a short while. Another purpose is to see whether the rate of progress they might afford in their organization matches your ambition. So, you need to give a safe response to that question. A plausible answer could be: "It's hard to predict what will happen in five years. But I will feel a sense of accomplishment if I am making an important contribution at work."

11- What motivates you?
If you have read the first chapter of this book: "Know Who You Truly Are", and if you have completed the self-assessment: "What Motivates Me At Work", then you must already have a fair idea on the elements of a job that motivate you more and make you more satisfied. In fact, you should use this knowledge about what motivates you as an important factor to weigh your career choices and evaluate potential jobs. Your answer to this question needs to take that knowledge into account, and at the same time, should be tailored to the realities of the job you are applying for. Whatever the things that motivate you are, don't directly mention "money". Even if that's the case, you can say something like: "I enjoy working in an environment where the more I put in, the more I gain in return."

12- How would your coworkers describe you?
Power words to use include: Assertive, Attentive, Caring, Committed, Confident, Conscientious, Creative, Direct, Energetic, Friendly, Hard Worker, Intelligent, Methodical, Motivated, Objective, Patient, Persistent, Reliable, Resourceful, Respectful, Sociable, Supportive, Tenacious, Trustworthy, and Wise.

Pick up the words that you agree with your entrusted colleagues are the closest ones to describe you, and be ready to support your choices with evidences.

13- What's your leadership style?
The best answer is to explain that you adapt your leadership style depending on the circumstances. Sometimes it's best to be the kind of a compassionate leader, while some other times it's best to focus solely on getting things done. Stress that you have always been able to get

your direct reports to do their best, and to meet or surpass their objectives.

14- How much money do you earn?
Answer precisely. Don't make it appear that you earn more than you do. That would be a terrible mistake. Sometimes, a new boss can manage to know what your previous employer paid you. If he or she learns that you lied, they can terminate you on the spot.

15- What are your salary expectations?
A bad answer is: "I'm OK with whatever you are willing to pay". It will reveal you are so option-less. Another bad answer is to give an unrealistically high number. It will reveal you are unprofessional. The research that you have conducted prior to the interview should help you figure out the right salary range for that job. When you give a number, state it with confidence, asserting that you believe it is commensurate with the contributions you will make. Refer to the next chapter "Negotiate Your Salary" for golden nuggets on the topic.

- **Brainteaser questions**: As for puzzle type questions, such as "Name 5 uses of a stapler without staple pins", they have no correct answers. The point behind asking these questions is to test a candidate's ability to think on their feet. Just stay cool and try to give a witty answer. Some candidates cleverly return back the challenge. For example, when a candidate was asked the question: "How would you weigh an airplane without a scale?", she responded: "With or without passengers?"

As for the market sizing questions, such as "How many potatoes (in kg) does McDonald's sell in a year in Egypt?", most of these questions are less about how much you know about the given market, producer, or product, and more about how you approach the problem. You need to demonstrate that you always adopt a structure, a framework, or a model when tackling problems.

To answer a question like the one about McDonald's, turn it into a simple mathematical model. Start by estimating the number of restaurants in the region. As for potatoes per restaurant, you could estimate the number of orders of fries per day, and then estimate the amount of potatoes (in kg) that go into each order.

- **Behavioral and situational questions**: These questions try to assess two kinds of skills: skills that relate to the job itself (e.g., negotiation skills, or leadership skills) and skills that have to do with the company's culture and its values and behavioral traits that it promotes as being essential to work (e.g., teamwork or innovative problem solving). The research that you have done on the skills required to do the job and on the company's culture will greatly help you identify the kind of skills that the interviewer will likely try to measure during the interview.

After identifying the skills to be measured, bring a pen and paper, and write down examples for exhibiting each skill, from your work experience, education, volunteer activities, and so on. Then revise each example in the story-like format: Problem-Action-Outcome.

Problem: the situation or the challenge that you faced, and what you were trying to achieve.

Action: what you did, why you did it, and what the alternatives were.

Outcome: the results of your action, whether it solved the problem, and what you have learned.

Here is a list of the most popular 50 behavioral questions:

Leadership:
   1. Tell me about a time when you accomplished something significant that wouldn't have happened if you had not been there to make it happen.

2. Tell me about a time when you were able to step into a situation, take charge, muster support and achieve good results.

3. Describe for me a time when you may have been disappointed in your behavior.

4. Tell me about a time when you had to discipline or fire a friend.

5. Tell me about a time when you've had to develop leaders under you.

Initiative and Follow-through:

6. Give me an example of a situation where you had to overcome major obstacles to achieve your objectives.

7. Tell me about a goal that you set that took a long time to achieve or that you are still working towards.

8. Tell me about a time when you won (or lost) an important contract.

9. Tell me about a time when you used your political savvy to push a program through that you really believed in.

10. Tell me about a situation that you had significant impact on because of your follow-through.

Thinking and Problem Solving:

1. Tell me about a time when you had to analyze facts quickly, define key issues, and respond immediately or develop a plan that produced good results.

2. If you had to do that activity over again, how would you do it differently?

3. Describe for me a situation where you may have missed an obvious solution to a problem.

4. Tell me about a time when you anticipated potential problems and developed preventative measures.

5. Tell me about a time when you surmounted a major obstacle.

Communication:
1. Tell me about a time when you had to present a proposal to a person in authority and were able to do this successfully.

2. Tell me about a situation where you had to be persuasive and sell your idea to someone else.

3. Describe for me a situation where you persuaded team members to do things your way. What was the effect?

4. Tell me about a time when you were tolerant of an opinion that was different from yours.

Working Effectively with Others:
1. Give me an example that would show that you've been able to develop and maintain productive relations with others, though there were differing points of view.

2. Tell me about a time when you were able to motivate others to get the desired results.

3. Tell me about a difficult situation with a co-worker, and how you handled it.

4. Tell me about a time when you played an integral role in getting a team (or work group) back on track.

Work Quality:
1. Tell me about a time when you wrote a report that was well received. What do you attribute that to?

2. Tell me about a time when you wrote a report that was not well received. What do you attribute that to?

3. Tell me about a specific project or program that you were involved with that resulted in improvement in a major work area.

4. Tell me about a time when you set your sights too high (or too low).

Creativity and Innovation:
   1. Tell me about a situation in which you were able to find a new and better way of doing something significant.

   2. Tell me about a time when you were creative in solving a problem.

   3. Describe a time when you were able to come up with new ideas that were key to the success of some activity or project.

   4. Tell me about a time when you had to bring out the creativity in others.

Priority Setting:
   1. Tell me about a time when you had to balance competing priorities and did so successfully.

   2. Tell me about a time when you had to pick out the most important things in some activity and make sure those got done.

   3. Tell me about a time that you prioritized the elements of a complicated project.

   4. Tell me about a time when you got bogged down in the details of a project.

Decision Making:
   1. Describe for me a time when you had to make an important decision with limited facts.

   2. Tell me about a time when you were forced to make an unpopular decision.

   3. Describe for me a time when you had to adapt to a difficult situation. What did you do?

4. Tell me about a time when you made a bad decision

5. Tell me about a time when you hired (or fired) the wrong person.

Ability to Work in Varying Work Conditions (stress, changing deadlines, etc.):
1. Tell me about a time when you worked effectively under pressure.

2. Tell me about a time when you were unable to complete a project on time.

3. Tell me about a time when you had to change work mid-stream because of changing organizational priorities.

4. Describe for me what you do to handle stressful situations.

Delegation:
1. Tell me about a time when you delegated a project effectively.

2. Tell me about a time when you did a poor job of delegating.

3. Describe for me a time when you had to delegate to a person with a full workload, and how you went about doing it.

Customer Service:
1. Tell me about a time when you had to deal with an irate customer.

2. Tell me about one or two customer-service related programs that you've done that you're particularly proud of.

3. Tell me about a time when you made a lasting, positive impression on a customer.

- **Case questions**: The best way to prepare for case questions is to solve as many cases as possible. You may Google the Case Interview Guide for "Harvard Business School, Management Consulting Club". It's a useful resource that includes 24 practice cases. Below are some general tips suggested by Mckinsey & Co., the largest consultancy firm in the world, to help you pass the case interview:

- Listen to the problem. Make sure you are answering the question that you have been asked.

- Begin by setting a structure. Think of four to five sub-questions that you need to answer before you can address the overall issue.

- Stay organized. When discussing a specific issue, remember why you are discussing it and where it fits into the overall problem.

- Communicate your train of thought clearly. If you have considered some alternatives and rejected them, tell the interviewer what and why.

- Step back periodically. Summarize what you have learned and what the implications appear to be.

- Ask for additional information when you need it. But make sure that the interviewer knows why you need the information.

- Watch for cues from the interviewer. Any information given to you by an interviewer is meant to help you - listen carefully and follow their lead.

- Be comfortable with numbers. You will almost always have to work with numbers in a case. This requires comfort with basic arithmetic and sometimes large quantities. You may also be asked to perform estimations.

- Don't fixate on "cracking the case." It is much more important to demonstrate a logical thought process than to arrive at the solution.

- Use business judgment and common sense.

- Relax and enjoy the process. Think of the interviewer as a teammate in a problem-solving process and the case as a real client problem that you need to explore and solve.

- Always focus on actionable recommendations.

3. Questions you should ask

Typically after the interviewer is done with their questions, they ask you: "Do you have any questions that you would like to ask me?" It's just as much important to ask the right questions as it was to provide the right answers. The benefit of questions you should ask the interviewer is twofold: first, you learn more about the job and the organization so that you know whether they are the right choice for you, and second, it's another chance to differentiate yourself from competition and show how professional you are.

You need to prepare 3-5 questions that are relevant to the job, department, management, and the organization. Here are a few questions to ask:

1. Do you provide any sort of professional development or training?

2. How do you measure employees' performance? And, how often?

3. Who was in this job before? And, why did they leave (if it's an already established job and not a new opening)?

4. Could you explain your organizational structure?

5. With whom will the successful candidate be working most closely? And, to whom will she/he be directly reporting?

6. How much experience do the team members possess?

7. What are the career progress opportunities offered to high performers?

8. Why do you enjoy working for this company?

9. What are the qualities of the most successful people in the organization?

10. If there is another interview, who is the next person/group I will be interviewing?

4. Dressing for the interview

The very initial impression the interviewer gets about you is determined by your appearance. And, a good deal of your appearance has to do with the way you dress. So, you need to dress in a way that stirs a positive impression upfront, and hence makes your job a bit easier for the rest of the interview.

Very simply, you must dress something clean, neat, and appropriate for the occasion. Dress formally. The best colors of your suit are Blue and Grey. Blue is a calming colour that evokes emotions of trust, loyalty, and peacefulness. Grey reflects sophistication and authority and is very suitable for corporate environment. Dangerous colours to avoid are Red and Orange. If the interviewer is going to be a female, pay close attention to details like your nails, your belt, your watch, and your haircut.

5. Interview mistakes to avoid

Here is a list of thing you can do ONLY if you wish to destroy your chances getting the job:

- Arriving late: learn more about time management in chapter 7: "Polish Your Skills". If it's impossible to make it on time, call the interviewer, apologize, and arrange to reschedule.

- Dressing inappropriately: enough said earlier about how you should dress for the interview.

- Having poor body language: lack of eye contact, nervous gestures, inconsistent facial expressions, quivering voice, crossing your arms, or using your hands too much while talking.

- Lying or faking stories: interviewers are trained to discover it, and it will hurt your image in the core.

- Talking too little or too much: being overly brief implies that you don't have enough to talk about. Also, elaboration doesn't mean going on and on or drifting away from the subject.

- Not answering the question: it triggers the alarm that you are either not prepared or not paying enough attention.

- Being arrogant: again, you must not confuse pride in yourself or accomplishments with arrogance. The former is a required trait. The latter is an immediate turn off.

- Acting rude or offensive: never lose your temper. One of the interviewer aims is to test your patience.

- Talking in a negative tone: victimizing yourself or badmouthing your former boss, company, or colleagues will surely backfire.

6. Following up on an interview

After the interview, it's advisable to send an email to thank the interviewer and appreciate their consideration for you. You need to send this follow up email within one day after the interview, so that they continue to remember you. And, even if you don't hear from the interviewer by the planned time for feedback, don't be afraid to phone them and refresh your interest in the job. After all, and regardless of whether you get the job or not, the interview itself was an excellent opportunity to get an exposure to influential people and to broaden your professional network. Who knows what other possibilities lie ahead?

Chapter 5: Negotiate Your Salary

In my early career, I got an offer for a dream job in one of a newly established multinational. I was offered the same salary I've asked for during the interview, so I was happy and I took the job. Few months later, I accidentally discovered that some other colleague with exactly the same qualifications, same job description, and the same hiring date, was getting 40% higher in salary than me! That was the time I've come to learn -the hard way rather than the soft way- few key lessons about salary negotiations, and realized that I must get this area in my life handled.

Salary negotiation is considered one of the key negotiations in everybody's life, and whether you are a job seeker or a current employee, it is usually one of the highly stressful situations you may go through, since many of your personal plans and aspirations revolve around how much money you make. Over this chapter, I will try to offer you some tips to guide you through your next salary or pay raise negotiation.

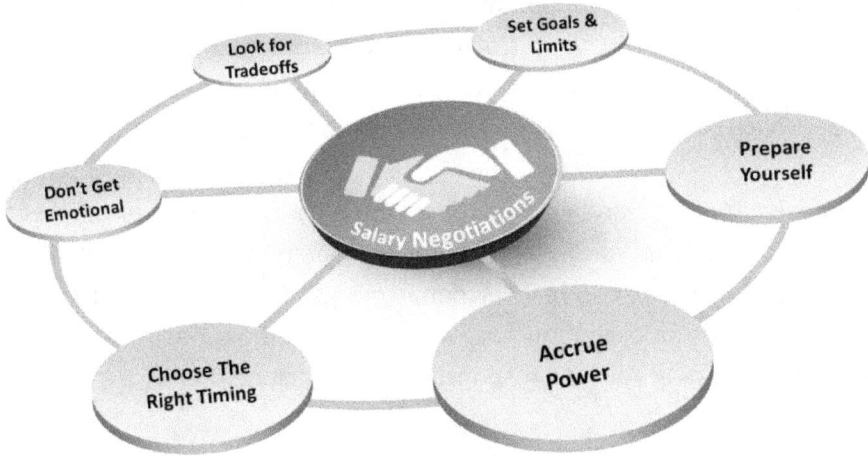

Figure 5.1   Tips of Salary Negotiations

1. Accrue a good deal of "power" well before approaching any salary negotiation

Many people falsely assume that they are powerless when it comes to negotiating their salaries. They get in the boss's office, get the "number", and then they get back to work. Perhaps this assumption stems from a basic premise about demand and supply, that there are many other workers out there who would happily and readily take that job for the same or even less money. This premise will not hold true if you make yourself a "hard-to-substitute" employee.

If you are already a high performer, you will have a good deal of power. As the renowned negotiating coach Jim Thomas explains in his book "Negotiate to Win", you have the power to be more committed and cooperative or just compliant, to do outstanding or merely ordinary work, to be resourceful and creative or spitefully conforming. You have the power to make your department look great or mediocre, to help your boss succeed or fail.

If you try to keep your skills up to date and to build your distinctive knowledge and expertise by engaging in new, challenging projects or assignments, joining multiple task forces, and making your organization substantially invest in your training and development, then you will become indispensable. You will not be a commodity and you will be able to approach salary negotiations from a position of power.

If you also try to expand your job description by doing more or different things, it may help you escape things like salary freeze, official salary range, one increase per year, or departmental limits. Because this is a job change, it's an exception. Discover things the boss needs done, and suggest expanding your job responsibilities to include them.

2. Prepare yourself and don't expect your boss to negotiate for you

Where money is concerned, your interests diverge somewhat from your employer's. To your employer, your payroll is still regarded as an expense rather than an investment, no matter how people-oriented the organizational culture is. Employers always wish to spend as little as possible to attract and retain the talent they need. Trusting your employer to fully "take care of you" in salary negotiations could be a costly mistake.

Prior to a salary discussion, prepare a comprehensive list of your past and future accomplishments and try to monetize them as much as possible. These are what determine your value as an employee, like specific contributions you make towards the organization's goals, additional revenues you induce, cost savings you bring about, or productivity of some work activities that you enhance. Gather all necessary documentations to prove your contributions and don't assume that your boss knows or remembers them. After all, you must also get prepared emotionally for the negotiation, for if you don't believe that you deserve a raise, nobody else will.

Get a grasp on the company's performance, and the overall industry prospects, as it wouldn't be a wise idea to ask for a raise if things in the environment are going really bad. Also, learn about the going rates for your job. As per Michael C. Donaldson in his engaging book "Negotiation for Dummies", to win a salary negotiation, you should know what a top salary is in your particular position. Just like you did in the reality check section of chapter 2, search websites like www.salaryexpert.com to see what people in positions similar to yours typically make. Ask your colleagues and recruitment agencies, check the classified ads, or even go out on some job interviews in other workplaces to get this information.

3. Set your goals and limits

The golden rule: "Aim high to get what you want" still works here. Remember that the first number you ask for sets the maximum that you can get. Your first number will probably be rejected, so it cannot be the minimum that you can accept. You have to keep a room to go down, avoid deadlocks, and let the boss save their face. Rehearse the number you will ask for until you can say it with confidence. Remember also that you still need to sound realistic. You want to ask things for which your boss or the hiring manager can realistically say yes, or you will come across as a fool or unprofessional.

Decide on your walk away point, which is the minimum amount you are willing to go for, and decide what you will do if the company does not meet your minimal expectations. You need to have a plan B, which can range from quitting on the spot (or turning down the offer if it's a new job), to start looking for another job, to just adapting and accepting the situation.

Even if you get a "No," don't give up. It's not forever. Push for a commitment to an early, specific date for a salary review. After all, be sure that you know who makes the final decision about salaries or raises in the company. If your boss or the hiring manager isn't the final decision maker, gain his or her trust first, and then ask them to represent your situation to the final decision maker.

4. Look for tradeoffs

If you meet firm resistance on salary, look for tradeoffs. Ask about other, non-salary elements of compensation, such as bonuses, overtime, flextime, health-club membership, child-care expense reimbursement, graduate or continuing education support, and the like. Your company might be more flexible on some of those options.

5. Don't use emotional appeal and never threaten your boss

Keep your emotions in check and build your case on objective evidence. There is nothing worse than trying to appeal emotionally to the boss or the hiring manager by saying things like you need the money to pay your own bills or to feed your kids. To management, only the organization's needs matter, and it's only the organization's needs that should be discussed.

Never threaten your boss that you will be quitting your job if you don't get what you want. It will surely backfire on you whatever your boss's response is. If your boss says "No", you will have to pack your stuff and leave on the spot, or stay and lose your face. If your boss says "Yes" to your request for the raise, you will still be regarded as a disloyal employee who cannot be fully trusted anymore.

It's only when you have received a firm, written offer from another employer that you can talk to your boss about your thought to leave. Don't even bring it to the discussion in a frame of arm twisting, but in a tactful frame of exploring career options with your boss, and allow them to prepare their response.

6. Remember that timing is very important

Where, when, and how you seat yourself to discuss a pay raise with your boss can impact the entire negotiation. Don't surprise your boss. Tell them in advance that you want to schedule a 30 minutes slot of uninterrupted time in their office to discuss your salary. There is no better opportunity to negotiate your salary than when you've just done something extraordinary. Immediately after you are awarded a big sales contract, completed a major project, or developed a new product, your boss will feel grateful, and your importance to the organization will never be clearer.

Chapter 6: Win The Race Of Your First 100 Days

Congratulations! You are hired, and you went out celebrating this major event in your life with your buddies. Now, you are back home and you find it hard to sleep from the excitement about this dream job you are going to start in a week or so. It is even getting nerve-racking.

You must be asking yourself what kind of things you must do right from the start to put you on the right track, because as career experts say, the first three months of any job are an extension of the interview process. In this chapter, I will show you how to nail your first 100 days in a new job, so that you will be destined for a long-term success.

Win The Race:

- Prepare For the Race
- Promote Yourself
- Organize Access To Information
- Accelerate Your Learning
- Break Free From Old Role's Psyche
- Align The Team
- Achieve Quick Wins
- Reconnect With Former Colleagues
- Assess Yourself
- Catch Your Breath

Figure 6.1   How to Win The Race of Your First 100 Days

1. Prepare for the race

You must spend the time from the moment you accepted the job till the moment you walk into the company's premises, to prepare for the race.

It's a race that you only win when you prove to yourself and to everyone that you were the best bet for the job.

In their book "You're in Charge - Now What?", Thomas J. Neff and James M. Citrin emphasize the same meaning when the say: "No serious athlete walks into a competition without prior preparation. It should be no different when you are approaching a challenging new business assignment. You too are entering a race." Here are the main things you need to do even before your day one on the job:

- Put a performance plan: Sit with your new boss to discuss and align on a plan for your first 100 days work objectives. It's very important that you know what he or she exactly expects you to learn, do, and deliver. This will greatly help you understand your priorities, opportunities, challenges, and timelines. Even if you are so enthusiastic to prove yourself, just don't forget about the golden rule: "Under promise and over deliver". Read the boss and understand his or her communication preferences and working style. You may refer to chapter 10: "Manage Your Boss" for further advices on that subject.

Your boss will appreciate your dedication and enthusiasm to get involved in the work even before your official start. He or she will probably also take you from your hand and introduce you to other key people in the department or the organization with whom you will be interacting.

- Elevate your knowledge: You may need to blow the dust off some old books or manuals and refresh any practical knowledge that will help you on the job. Check also with your boss if your new company offers complimentary classes to help employees get up to speed on both technical (hard) skills and soft skills, and see the possibility to sign up for the ones that you need. If it is not possible to take these classes before you officially start working for the company, then at least try to take those that may be available online for independent study.

- Improve your physical conditioning: Being in good shape will boost your brain power, will give you the discipline you need to perform well under pressure, and will generally make you more self-confident. Look after your body. Exercise more frequently to raise your stamina and improve your blood flow. Also, depending on the demands of your new role, you may need to perform some health checks prior to starting the race.

- Help your family adjust: Your family needs to be prepared emotionally just as much as you do, especially if the new job represents a significant transition in your professional life and will require you -at least initially- to spend more hours in office. Also if your new job involves relocating, you may decide to leave your family behind for the first few weeks or even months, if this will minimize their turmoil and enable you to focus more.

2. Promote yourself

Starting day one, take the initiative to meet new people in the workplace. Don't settle in your desk and wait for people to approach you. Start with the group that is closest to you, the people you are directly working with. Practice your story, and at every opportunity, explain who you are, what you do, and what your background is. If you are transiting into a leadership role, you may also need to explain why you took the job and what you plan to achieve.

There may be some challenges about why you got the job over other people in the same team. In such case, prepare a clear explanation that outlines your strengths without putting down others (e.g., "I have been studying for a project management diploma while working. I also have participated in all our major projects over the past 2 years, and have attended all the available trainings, so that I could be ready to move up. It is important for all us to keep up with our education and skills. I would be happy to help you figure out what you need to do to get there.") This will help others settle down and work productively.

3. Organize your access to information

One trick to ramping up at a new job is to be able to easily access the information you need. Make sure your how-to instructions and various lists are well-organized. If your job requires some moving around, it's no good to have a Post-it back on your bulletin board. Use a portable notebook or accordion folder with labeled dividers that you can even take home for review.

4. Accelerate your learning

Learning should be a primary focus for your first 30 days on the job. Absorb your job's technical aspects, assimilate the culture and the jargon of the workplace, learn the established policies as well as the unwritten rules, identify key players, and decode office politics, so that you can fit in the mold and quickly overcome any possible "reality shocks".

Don't undermine the power of your "fresh eyes". Teams routinely fail to see flaws in their processes which are very often noticed by newcomers who bring a fresh perspective. Don't hesitate to address things that seem illogical to you, and keep in mind that there is no such thing as a dumb question when you are new to a job. Identify and befriend those who can help you learn all you need to know. Always figure out the right question, the right person, and the right time to ask.

Your new workplace has factored in time for your learning curve. When working in a fast-paced environment, you may feel pressured to catch up quickly. However, and as another golden rule, you must always look as if everything you do is easy. Don't break a sweat or show you are exerting a great effort. Especially when you are about to faint, appear to be full of energy and ready for another course.

Maintain the balance between time and quality of your work. If you do new tasks too fast or make rash decisions, you're liable to commit mistakes, which will hit your credibility. On the other hand, if you take too much time to complete something or do too much analysis before taking decisions, you may come across as inefficient or indecisive. If you find it difficult to find a point of balance, consult your boss and communicate your appreciation of the importance of getting things done correctly and timely.

5. Break free from the psyche of your old role

The very same habits or behaviors that worked for you and helped your success in the past, can actually hinder your performance in your new role. For example, one team leader used to be deeply committed to nurturing his or her team, yet, in a new workplace, this behavior might be seen as playing favorites. Another example is a supervisor who very often chooses to mull over suggestions of team members before making decision, yet, in a different work setting, he or she might be labeled as "unresponsive".

As Marshall Goldsmith claims in his book: "What Got you Here Won't Get You There", one of the greatest mistakes of successful people is the assumption: "I am successful. I behave this way. Therefore, I must be successful because I behave this way!" The key point here is to put the past behind you and learn how to adapt your working style to match the norms of the new environment. Identify which behaviors are encouraged in the new workplace and learn and practice them, and also identify which behaviors are discouraged, and "unlearn" and stop doing them.

6. Align the team

If your new role involves leading a team, assess the team you've inherited, identify weak links or people who are in the wrong positions. Think of five or six questions that you will ask every member of your team. The questions show people that you care enough to listen and pinpoints which issues you care about.

Create a plan, in liaison with your boss, for addressing personnel issues within six months. Assess each team member based on competence, judgment, energy, focus, relationships and trust. Recognize good performers to enhance the morale of the team. Consider factors like previous appraisals, skills, responses to probing questions, and verbal and nonverbal cues.

Work with your team to set team and individual goals and performance metrics. Reevaluate duties, responsibilities, processes, procedures, team dynamics, and communication and reporting methods. Develop a plan to implement any necessary changes.

7. Achieve quick wins

While focusing on your long term success, you should also achieve some early wins during your first 100 days to build credibility and gain momentum. Secure some early wins so people will believe in your ability to achieve. In his book: "The First 90 Days", Michael Watkins argues that if you don't create a few landmarks on the way, the journey can get less encouraging. Establish several achievable short-term goals, and advertise your successes.

8. Reconnect with former colleagues

Even though you might be deeply immersed in the errands of your new job, don't forget to find the time to reach out to colleagues from your previous job. Pay a visit to your old company and reconnect with people over there or at least keep in touch with them by phone. The best time to refresh your connections is when you don't need anything.

9. Assess yourself

Week by week, monitor your progress on what you learn, do, and achieve against the original plan that you have put before day one. Adjust your objectives as necessary to make sure they remain realistic. Honestly appraise your skills, abilities and weaknesses you bring to the job. Make sure you capitalize on your strengths, while taking timely actions to improve your weak points. Seek mentorship when needed.

10. Catch your breath before continuing the race

If your first 100 days are a sprint, then your long-term tenure in the new job is a marathon. After a sprint, an athlete needs to take a quick breather before resuming the race. So do you. After you finish your first 100 days take a short vacation, if possible, or take a whole weekend, and do some recreational activity to reenergize your body and empty your brain. Then you'll be in shape for continuing the marathon.

Chapter 7: Make A Difference

Once, a man was walking along a beach. Off in the distance he could see a person going back and forth between the surf's edge and the beach. As the man approached, he could see that there were thousands of starfish stranded on the sand as a result of the action of the tide. Many of them were sure to perish. He found this person continuing the task of picking up starfish one by one and throwing them into the surf.

He came up to the person and said: "You must be crazy. There are hundreds of miles of beach covered with starfish. You can't possibly make a difference." The person looked at the man. He then stooped down and picked up one more starfish and threw it back into the ocean. He turned back to the man and said: "It sure made a difference to that one!"

The moral of the story, written by Loren Eiseley under the name "The Star Thrower", is that even the smallest contribution can create a significant difference. As far as work and careers are concerned, you cannot truly lead a fulfilling career unless you try to make a difference by conquering a challenge, solving a problem, and leaving a mark at every venue. A big salary, lofty job title, fancy office, and creative perks may all make you happy about your workplace. But, to be happy about your own self and about the kind of work that you do, you must have a meaningful contribution that makes a difference.

For any role that you assume or assignment that you take, you need to dwell on the basic question: "What difference will I make?" It may help you answer that question to conceive of things like your knowledge, expertise, or even character that will make people come to you. Things you wish those people will remember you with. Here is the recipe:

Figure 7.1   The Recipe of Making a Difference

1. Approach your job as a volunteer

Try to see your daily work as your personal contribution, so you can make the mental shift from being an "employee" to acting as if you are a "volunteer." In their book "Great Work, Great Career", Stephen R. Covey and Jennifer Colosimo argue that this shift is vital to forging a great career, as the volunteer approaches a task with the clarity and sense of purpose that flows from willingness and passion to help a great cause.

Having the attitude of a volunteer will shape your behavior in ways that are highly desirable by employers. It will make you go the extra mile to get things done, suggest new ideas, and get out of your way to help other people. It will help you contribute the right way at work, become indispensable and eventually reap many rewards, including the gratification of doing the things that matters to you.

2. Hone your talents

Your talents (the sum of your skills, abilities, and knowledge) make you a unique person with unique contribution in your field. Your means of production in this knowledge-based economy is no longer a machine or an equipment. It's your brains. Analyze the portfolio of skills, abilities, and knowledge required to effectively do your job, and benchmark yours against it. Strive then to bridge all existing skill or knowledge gaps. Tackle these gaps in a prioritized fashion. For instance, if you are a web developer, then you need to make sure you master the knowledge of HTML5, SQL, and JavaScript before thinking to sign up for a class on running effective negotiations.

Beside the job-specific skills required to do a particular job, there are four "survival skills" that cut across almost all jobs, working levels, and sectors. Those skills are: emotional intelligence, communication skills, problem solving skills, and time management skills. You must ensure you possess these skills at least to the extent that satisfies your job requirements. If you wish to figure out where you currently stand with regard to each of these skills, take the below self-assessments:

What's My Emotional Intelligence? (Pg. 148)

What's My Communication Style? (Pg. 151)

How Good Am I At Problem Solving? (Pg. 158)

How Good Am I At Time Management? (Pg. 163)

3. Make your own luck

Having the right mindset and the right talents is a necessary but not sufficient prerequisite for contributing significantly and making a difference. Luck can be a critical factor in the equation. We all know that. But, highly successful people know a couple of more things. They know that luck is not a completely random phenomenon, and they also know how to influence their own luck. They believe that luck is as much about attitude as it is about probability.

In their book: "Heart, Smarts, Guts, and Luck", Anthony K. Tjan and his coauthors interviewed hundreds of successful professionals and found that those who seem luckier than others have two characteristics in common. They possess the "lucky attitude" and they build the "lucky network".

The lucky attitude stems from three traits: 1) humility that leads them to realize that they don't have all the answers or all the solutions, 2) curiosity that drives them to search for answers and solutions by experimenting with new ideas and ventures, and 3) optimism that encourages them to carry on and believe that something better is always possible. It seems that luck is a self-fulfilling prophecy: more luck tends to come to those who believe in possibility.

To double their chances, those people also build their lucky networks based on openness and generosity rather than on a specific targeting of must-have relationships. They just tend to be able to "bump" into the right people at the right time. A case study published by Harvard Business School about Rachel Ray, the American celebrity chef, reveals that she was able to make her own luck, and launch her massively successful television career in 2001, when the NBC's Today show had a rash of guest cancellations due to a snowstorm. One of the producers had been given Ray's cookbook as a gift and suggested she fills in. She drove nine hours through the snow to make it to the studio. Next day she was offered a $360,000 contract with the Food Network.

4. Be the team player who is in demand

You can hardly accomplish any major success alone. To contribute, you almost always need to work with other teammates. Teams are an essential element in the fabric of today's business organizations, and managers are usually on the look for those who can be good team players rather than those who seek to be a prima donna all the time. Honing your individual skills doesn't compensate for any lack in your teamwork skills. You must spend time on developing both, just as a soccer player who must spend his or her training time on mastering both individual, technical skills, and team/group tactics within their lines on the field. Best team players are known to possess many qualities, but the most vital ones are:

- **Cooperative**: They see other members of the team as coworkers not competitors. They put aside suspicion, focus on the group, and celebrate collective wins.

- **Dependable**: They live up to their obligations as individuals and as team member. They strive to consistently meet their responsibilities, show good judgment, and contribute steadily.

- **Flexible**: They can adapt themselves to working with different groups of people and under various conditions. They can feel more comfortable learning new things or tasks.

- **Communicative**: They seek to clearly understand their assignments, instructions, and priorities. They communicate directly and openly with other team members. They pay extra attention to tense relationships and don't let them worsen.

- **Disciplined**: They are able to do what is required from them, whether they like it or not. They strive to master their thought and their emotions, and they take responsibility for making things happen.

- **Selfless**: They subordinate their own interests to those of the team. They are generous and loyal to their teammates, and they avoid political quarrels.

5. Act ethically, always

Acting ethically means to know what's right and what's wrong from a moral perspective, and only do the right things like keeping concern for others, being truthful, fulfilling commitments, and striving for fairness. The benefit of this for you is that you will "do well by doing good". You will protect your reputation and self-esteem, and will avoid lots of stress, let alone facing any potential legal consequences in extreme cases. By acting ethically and considering the interests of others, you ultimately serve your own self-interest.

People do wrong for various reasons that include pressure for success or pressure by peers, false claim of entitlement, thinking that rules do not apply to them, not viewing the act as illegal, and lacking of resources. To be confident any of your actions does not cross the border of morality, ask yourself these questions:

- Would I accept it if someone else did the same action to me? Or if they did it to someone else?

- Would I be comfortable telling my best friend about my action?

- Would I be comfortable if my action was publicized in a newspaper or on television?

- Long after I do it, would I want to look back in hindsight and be comfortable with my action?

Chapter 8: Impress Others

In the past chapter, we have discussed how to make a difference in what you do. Over this chapter, we will discuss how to make other people realize that you, yourself, are different. In every new encounter, be it wanting to pass a job interview, completing a sales deal, or networking with new people at some gathering, you always seek to leave a good first impression. The power of first impressions is that they usually last, and there is a good reason for that: In this fast-paced life, we are typically too busy to give a second chance. Our brains try to economically process the loads of information they are exposed to, so the time window we leave open to judge someone or something is short, and once we create a perception, we stick to it and it becomes hard to change.

Creating a positive impression simply means that you need to actively manage both how people "feel" about you, and how they "think" about you. There are hundreds of books, articles, and videos on how to impress others, but many of them lack the proper balance between these two components. Some resources accentuate the importance of building rapport and excellent communication (the "feeling" component), while some others favor the presentation of your achievements or the solution you'll bring to a business problem (the "thinking" component). Here, I'll attempt to offer an integrative approach that can help you make powerful impressions in your first encounters.

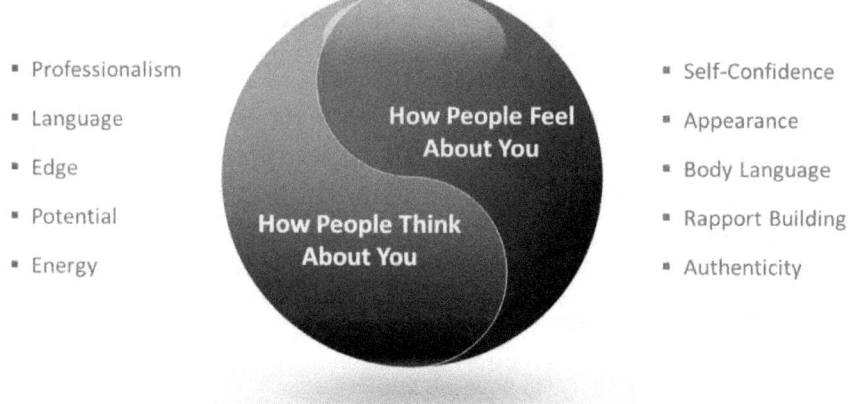

- Professionalism
- Language
- Edge
- Potential
- Energy

How People Feel About You

How People Think About You

- Self-Confidence
- Appearance
- Body Language
- Rapport Building
- Authenticity

Figure 8.1   What Makes a Powerful First Impression

1. Manage how people "feel" about you:

Just within few seconds after you first meet someone, and even before you say a word, they form an initial impression about you. Research shows that your appearance and body language carry around 80% of the information people need to form that impression. Again, our brains are wired so that initial impressions, which are mostly emotional, can subconsciously cloud rational judgments (for more information, Google Paul D. MacLean's theory on brain evolution and Daniel Goleman's concept of brain hijacking). That is why you must manage how people feel about you before you manage how they think about you. Here are the areas you must handle:

- **Self-confidence**: Can you name one reason why others would have confidence in you when you don't seem to have confidence in yourself? It's that simple and it all starts here. To have self-confidence, you must have good self-image and self-talk, and belief in your skills and abilities. It's a long journey that requires you to work on yourself first before any attempt to influence how people see you. That journey starts when you set meaningful, yet not necessarily so hard, goals in any aspect of your life (e.g. learning new stuff, passing some test, or stopping a bad habit), and devote enough time and sincere effort to achieving them. With every success in achieving a goal, your self-confidence will grow, you'll be motivated to set and achieve harder goals, and that cycle will go on. Nothing here can be more inspirational than what Henry Ford once said: "Whether you think you can, or you think you cannot - you're actually right".

- **Appearance**: You need to be well groomed. Remember that looking good is more important than being good looking, and it helps boost your self-confidence. As we said earlier in chapter 4: "Master The Job Interview Process", you don't need to wear expensive brands but you must be clean, dress neatly, know how to match styles, pick colours that go together, and always pay enough attention to details. It's ok to get a professional advice from a stylist or a fashion TV show.

- **Body language**: Your body is constantly sending out signals that reflect your internal state without you even being aware of it. Other people can read cues from things like your facial expressions, eye contact, hand shaking, gestures, postures, and voice tone, to learn things like whether you feel confident, nervous, bored, interested, or relaxed. Allan Pease offers a comprehensive guide to master this universal language in his book: "Body Language, How to read others' thoughts by their gestures". Become aware of your body language and constantly monitor it, and you'll guarantee powerful initial impressions. Practice enough to make sure your body language is naturally asserting and complementing your spoken words. Maintain an open stance, such as open arms and open legs, to demonstrate confidence and comfort. After all, the way you say something can be more important than what you say.

- **Rapport building**: This is the art of connecting with others. First, recall people's names and use them in the conversation. That's a sweet way to show your care. Shake hands warmly, smile authentically and slowly, and keep eye contact while speaking. Prepare few strategies for starting conversations and breaking the ice. Your topics should be appropriate for the occasion and level of intimacy. Choose subjects that others can relate to, so they feel comfortable sharing their stories in return. Practice humor, storytelling, and sincere compliments as great tools that help you connect with people and tap into their feelings. Make others feel like the center of attention and listen to them carefully. Read their body language, mirror their gestures, and match their mood and vocal pattern. More on that subject will come in the next chapter: "Build Your Professional Network".

- **Authenticity**: Always be yourself and never pretend to be someone else. Don't act overconfidently, or you'll come across as insecure. Don't overdo any of the above advices, or you might be seen as trying too hard. Finally, make your motives and intent clear in order to instill trust.

2. Manage how people "think" about you:

Now you're done with disarming the other person "emotionally", and it's time to show them "rationally" the value you'll bring them or their business. In other words, while the first part of the chapter was concerned about your likeability as a person, the second part will focus on how to present your competence. The mindset you need to espouse here is to market yourself as if you were a brand that signifies distinctive qualities. Here are the things you need to take care of:

- **Professionalism**: The fastest way people judge your professionalism is through your timeliness. Do your best to be sharply always on time, for this will convey a clear message about your good sense of time management, professionalism, and ability to fulfill your commitments. If -for any reason- you'll be running late for an appointment, call to apologize before the due time, explain the reason for your delay, and ask for rescheduling. Another measure of professionalism is ethics and work morale. So, abandon any negative tone in talking about your previous company, ex-boss, colleagues or competitors.
- **Language**: Adopt a vivid and simple language, employ relevant metaphors to stir inspiration, and learn the secrets of framing from L.

Michael Hall in his book "mind-lines" to exert influence while adding charm to your conversations. Avoid using buzzwords and clichés statements, and try to find substitutes for overworked words like "nice", "smart", and "good". Don't use technical jargon, unless you are certain that the other person knows it already.

- **Edge**: This is the sum of your strengths; what you are excellent at and what makes you stand out. Remember that back in chapter 3: "Write A Resume That Makes Your Phone Rings", we said that you must not think of your strengths and talents in isolation, but in relation to how you can employ them to solve the employer's or customer's specific business problems. This requires you to do your homework and learn everything you can about the firm you're approaching. Being uninformed will reflect poorly on your own image.

In their book "Great Work, Great Career", Stephen R. Covey and Jennifer Colosimo urge you to write a "contribution statement" that gives others a reason to hire you or to do business with you. A statement that pretty much resembles the "personal brand statement" that you need for your resume. For example, if you're a facility manager applying for a manufacturing company job, instead of saying that you seek *"a fulfilling position for using your communication and negotiation skills."* You can much more compellingly state: *"The costs of facility rentals eat up your company's profits. Drawing on my experience in lease management, I believe I can cut rental expenses by 10% to 20% by renegotiating contracts."*

- **Potential**: A surprising secret to marketing yourself is that people tend to be more impressed by candidates with high potential more than candidates with proven track record! Although this seems to be counter-intuitive, it is actually confirmed by a study conducted in 2012 by Stanford University and Harvard Business School, where evaluators were found to prefer -consciously or subconsciously- those who could be "the next big thing", over those who have already made their records or their names. Based on this finding, you must alter your approach to employers and clients: focus more on your future than on your past, even if your past was already impressive.

- **Energy**: If edge and potential are your engine, energy will be the fuel needed to power up this engine. It's the motive and the drive to constantly achieve and outperform. Enthusiasm and motivation are essential qualities that companies are seeking in today's more than ever competitive environment. Spark energy in your body language and your words, and remember that a good deal of your energy comes from taking the time for self-renewal.

Chapter 9: Build Your Professional Network

In more than one place in this book, it has been iterated that your professional network is by far your second greatest asset, just comes after your skills. Some career counselors even put it as the number one success factor. An effective professional network equates to more opportunities and faster progress. I have personally seen it many times that two employees can have similar skills and qualifications, but the one who moves up quicker is the one who knows more people and is a better networker. You probably also have noticed that when people need a doctor, a lawyer, a tax accountant, or so, they usually either go to someone they already know, or someone who has been recommended to them.

Networking is becoming an essential feature of today's work environment, and according to Simone L. Andersen in her book "Networking - A Professional Discipline", more than 60% of all job vacancies are filled through networking and recommendations. But, it usually takes years to build a solid professional network. So, whether you are a student, a job seeker, an employee, or an entrepreneur, you must not procrastinate on starting to build your own network.

Networking requires being generous with your time and connections in a process of continuous giving and taking; the worst time to start is when you need something. Bear in mind that the effectiveness of your network is a matter of both breadth (spread) of your connections, and quality (strength and relevance) of these connections, so here is how to build, expand and maintain your professional network.

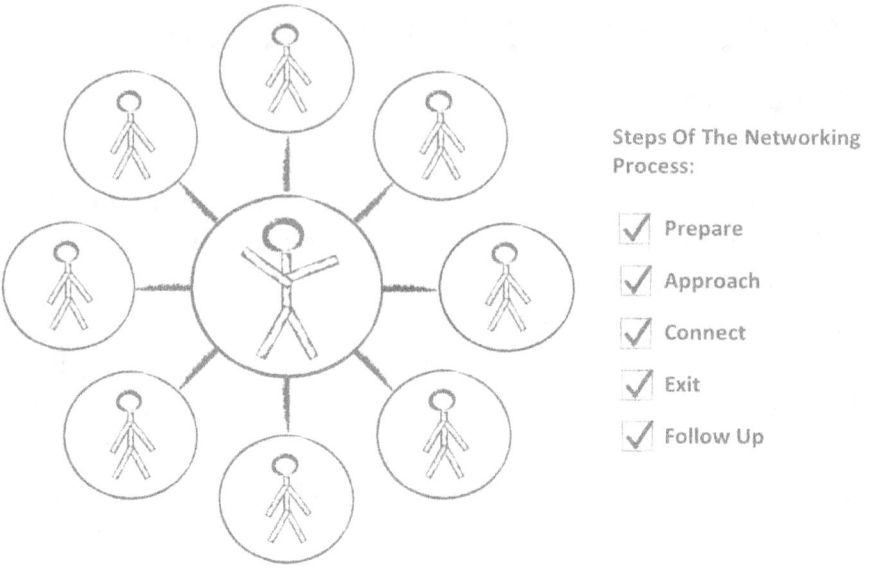

Steps Of The Networking Process:

- ✓ Prepare
- ✓ Approach
- ✓ Connect
- ✓ Exit
- ✓ Follow Up

Figure 9.1   Steps of The Networking Process

1. Pursue relevant networking opportunities

If you remember at the time you were writing your career goals (Pg. 174), you needed to think about people who would support you achieve these goals. To be able to identify those people more precisely, try to chart the networks you are involved in today. When you first visualize this, you will find that you are involved in more than what you thought. You will be able to answer these questions more clearly:

- What active networks do I currently have?
- Can people in those networks help me achieve my career goals?
- Do I need to expand my networks and connect with new people who can help me get there?

Then think about how you adjust or expand your networks so that they support your career goals. You need to realize that networking requires being generous with your time, expertise, and connections in a process of continuous giving and taking. The worst time to start is when you need something, so plan for your networking requirements early enough.

Excellent opportunities to network and mingle with other professionals and businesspeople can be found by attending training courses, conferences, tradeshows, job fairs, alumni gatherings, parties, and volunteering and other social occasions. You can even enjoy wider access to attendees, guests, and speakers of these events if you help organizing them. Try also to locate and get introduced to the "Super-Connectors". Those are the few persons that Keith Ferrazzi and Tahl Raz describe in their book: "Never Eat Alone", as the gateways that link to other networks. They serve as the conduits to most other people.

2. Learn the art of networking

Networking is a social skill that anybody can learn. And just as it is for any other skill, practice makes perfect. So, before the very next networking opportunity looms, try to assimilate the below five steps of the networking process:

- **Prepare**: gather enough information about the event and the group of participants. Plan your behavior and the outcomes you anticipate by considering the below action points:

- Learn the specific terminology and phrases (jargon) used by the people or group you are going to meet. This will help you seamlessly tune in to their conversations.

- Find out the hot, provocative topics or issues pertinent to this group. Gain knowledge about these issues by skimming trade journals, searching the internet, or talking to insiders. Brining up these issues to the conversations will enrich the exchange.

- Identify the best thing you can offer. Check how you can help these attendees with your know-how, or by introducing them to others in your network.

- Draw mental images of how you should enter the room and how you should approach people.

- Who would be worthwhile new contacts that you can get out of the event.

Rehearsal is of paramount importance to your success at the event. Winston Churchill's contemporaries saw him as a fantastic conversationalist and dinner guest, yet he used to take hours in preparation for gatherings, rehearsing the comments and jokes he would share with specific people.

- **Approach**: initiating contact with strangers is frequently reported as one of the major causes of social anxiety. People feel this anxiety for reasons that are mostly related to either fear of rejection or lack of self-confidence. This is why people attending social events often keep talking to people they know and never wind up with a new acquaintance. If you experience the same anxiety when approaching strangers, then you need to realize that your fear is typically irrational. Very few people will actually reject you for initiating a conversation. Most will be grateful to the person who starts an exchange. So take the risk and assume the burden of initiating the conversation, especially if you consider the potential benefits it entails. And, as mentioned earlier, doing mental rehearsal prior to the event will bolster the self-confidence you need.

If you don't have someone to introduce you to other people at the event, start by looking for an "approachable person," someone who isn't talking with another person or group. This person might be sitting alone or perusing the buffet. Make eye contact and smile. If the individual responds, greet him or her, and introduce yourself. When you get the person's name, use it early on in the conversation. This will help you not forget the name. Besides, it will help build rapport quickly, since people love to be called by their names.

Don't take your eyes off of the person you are talking to. Maintain perfect eye contact while you speak with him or her. Pay them an undivided attention, and align your whole body towards them. To provoke a sensation of similarity and make the other person feels more comfortable with you on a subconscious level, Leil Lowndes advises in her book: "How To Talk To Anyone", that you subtly match your conversational partner's gestures. But don't overdo it or you will surely offend. Also, grab the special words and phrases that he or she uses to describe something, and "Echo" your partner by using those words yourself.

Attend to the conversation prepared with a few "Icebreakers", or conversation starters. Classical topics (e.g., the weather or the place you are in, the occasion, the food, or special guests) still work fine. When you ask questions, make them open-ended questions that require more than one-word answer (e.g., what brings you here? What do you do?). Keep current with what's going on in the world or society, so that you can be ready to talk about things like TV programmes, Headlines in the media, culture, movies, and books.

These warm-up conversations are called "small talk" in some cultures. It is the kind of talk that happens between two people who don't know each other. It helps establish rapport and make a positive impression. Small talk gives us space to see the potential in a conversation and at the same time gives us the opportunity either to accept or to decline a relationship. That's why they say: "small talk is big". After all, remember that the way you say something is at least as important as what you say.

Mistakes to avoid while conversing include excessive argumentation, interrogative questions, interrupting your partner, monopolizing the conversation, acting superior, and criticism. Those are conversation killers and they undoubtedly leave a bad impression.

- **Connect**: Connecting with someone simply means to make them like you. When you "connect" with a person, he or she identifies with you in a way that increases your influence upon them. Connecting is about finding common grounds. You can do that if you focus on the other party, show genuine interest in their needs and what they feel important. Great salespeople know that nobody wants to be "sold", but everyone wants to be "helped". Instead of looking for people to help you, begin to help others. To earn support, you must give support. To get people on your side, quickly get on their side. This will signal an unselfish attitude that the other person will reciprocate.

To gain the trust of others, share something about yourself that is comfortable, positive and uncontroversial. Your topics should be appropriate for the occasion and level of intimacy. Mention subjects others can relate to so they feel comfortable sharing their stories in return. Relate authentic personal experiences they can share, feel and respect.

Be a good listener, and encourage others to talk about themselves. Attentive listening has three components: visual (by making eye contact, projecting receptive body language, and nodding), verbal (by paraphrasing the speaker's words to confirm that you heard correctly), and mental (by asking reflective or clarifying questions, processing what you've heard and retaining its essence). Many professionals are familiar with the techniques of the first two components of attentive listening much more than the third one. They show that they are overtly attentive visually, and verbally, but they are not really paying genuine attention. Truly listening to someone is what you need if you really wish to connect with them.

Use stories tactfully. To truly influence someone, don't simply provide facts and data. Instead, tell a story. Story gives people enough space to think for themselves. Whether your story is true or fictitious, use added emotional details to flesh out the facts. Consider how you use gestures, facial expressions, body language, pauses and voice tone to amplify the emotion you want to convey. Good storytellers are always on the lookout for wonderful stories. Annette Simmons, in her book: "The Story Factor", asserts that any event that creates an emotion or happens because of an emotion can become a story. She advises that when you search for a story, look for patterns, consequences, lessons, or utility. The only way to become a great storyteller is by telling stories. Practice often and develop a keen appreciation for the stories you hear.

Sincere compliments can be a very powerful tool to show appreciation to the other person and to connect with them. Compliments fall into three categories: appearance, possessions or behavior. Say something nice about what people are wearing, something they are carrying or something they did. Avoid being overly personal and understand that a praise that does not appear genuine will certainly backfire.

- **Exit**: you don't want to spend the whole time with just one person. You need to circulate and acquaint yourself with as many attendees as you can. So, give each person ten minutes of conversation. When leaving, don't make false excuses. Politely say: "I do need to get around and say 'hello' to the other people at this meeting." Exchange business cards, and write a few words on the back to remind you about that contact later.

End each conversation on a positive note. Smile and give a firm handshake. If you feel that you need more than ten-minute conversation, invite that person to a separate meeting or arrange with them for a phone call. You might say, "I don't want to monopolize your time here. Can we arrange to meet later?"

- **Follow up**: A meeting without a follow-up produces nothing. Follow-ups solidify personal connections and make it easier for people to remember you when you call them back later. Send an e-mail or make a phone call within one day after your initial contact. Convey how much you enjoyed your conversation and try to arrange another meeting. For a second contact, offer something concrete: a cup of coffee, a dinner, or an offer. Extend help to your new acquaintance, instead of recalling what he or she offered to do for you.

3. Maintain your network

In building a network, remember: above all, never, ever disappear. Stay accessible and noticeable. Maintain a purposeful social calendar to regularly keep in touch with your contacts. The Egyptian iconic singer Abdel-Halim Hafez (who is considered one of the great four of Arab music, and who left a legacy of hundreds of songs that are still enjoyed by millions of audience, thirty years after his death) was known not only for his rare, passionate voice, or his discipline, but also for his remarkable social intelligence. One of Abdel-Halim's close friends recited that he used to wake up every day, ask his house manager about those who phoned him that day, and starts by calling back those who did not phone him.

You need also to realize that your relational capital will not depreciate if you help new acquaintances get access to some influential, key persons in your own network. First, this access could be beneficial to both of them. Second, when you help someone, you benefit from access to their own network, which represents a geometric expansion of opportunities, ideas, and connections for you and for others.

4. Exploit the power of social media

As you meet new people, reinforce your relationships by finding and connecting with them on electronic social networks like LinkedIn, Facebook, or Twitter. Electronic social networks also represent an enticing opportunity to reach and connect with much more people and groups that you have never met in reality. To get the highest pay off out of your social media presence, consider the following points:

- Identify the platforms that make the most sense to your industry, and join or start relevant forums or discussion groups.

- Make sure that your social network profiles are updated and that they reflect your professional self.

- Be careful about consistency. What you write about yourself must remain similar across the all profiles and platforms.

- Remain active. LinkedIn product management team found that members who share content on LinkedIn at least once a week, are nearly 10 times more likely to be contacted for new opportunities than inactive people.

- Configure the notification settings on the different platforms so that you can track important activities of your connections and check how well your updates are being received.

Chapter 10: Manage Your Boss

Managing your boss is a skill that is sometimes overlooked. However, it is just as important as the skills of managing your subordinates, or managing your client relationships. Whether you are an entry-level employee or a corporate executive, mastering the skill of building an effective and healthy work relationship with your boss is crucial to your career success and advancement. This chapter will present you with eight key advices on how to manage your boss:

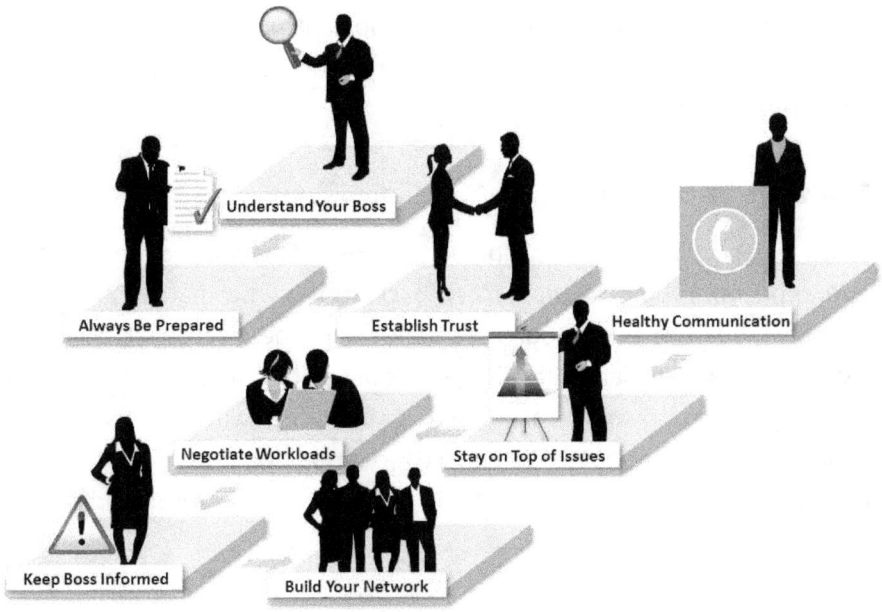

Figure 10.1   The Eight Advices to Managing Your Boss

1. Understand your boss

Start by paying enough effort to understand your boss's organizational and personal objectives, commitments, pressures, strengths and weaknesses, and preferred work style and communication style. Trying to see the world from the eyes of your boss and realizing what they are going through helps you better understand their motives and decisions. Staying self-centered will not get you anywhere with your boss.

Whether your boss is detail oriented, action oriented, or outcome oriented, you need to make sure all your interactions with them (discussions, presentations, reports, etc.) fit their preferences. If your boss is a "listener", brief them in person and then follow up with a memo. If they are a "reader", cover important points of your communication in a memo or a report, and then discuss them.

Finally, you know that timing is very important. Know the best time to approach your boss to discuss an issue or request something, in order to avoid rejection or procrastination.

2. Always be prepared

Prepare for all meetings and presentations. Know the needed details, and send your boss all necessary background information and brief agendas ahead of time. Your boss will neither be interested, nor have the time to analyze and filter huge amounts of data and statistics. It is your job to do so and present him or her only with the useful and actionable information. To avoid overloading your boss with information, ask yourself "What's in it for them?" before sending out any piece of information.

Ensure all your resource requests are backed up with rational and comprehensive justifications. Again, this is not only to secure your boss's approval, but also to protect your own credibility.

Prepare a list of key points before you talk to the boss and always begin discussions with the end in mind. State and clarify the objectives of the discussion before drowning into details.

3. Establish trust

Treat your boss with respect no matter what you feel about them. Don't complaint about your boss to others. Play to your boss's strengths and downplay their weaknesses. Support them in doing what they themselves are good at. It's a far more productive approach to build on their strengths, than trying to remedy their limitations. As Peter Drucker says in his masterpiece business book "Management", never underrate your boss, for it may cost you your job.

4. Maintain healthy communication

Ensure you meet regularly with your boss Keep them apprised of what you and your team are doing. Remember that "shameless bragging" about your achievements is needed to build their confidence in you. Don't whine! Your boss will hate it if you complaint every time they see you. However, it's completely fair to bring an objective complaint or an issue to the boss. just keep it professional and make sure you control your emotions.

Express some sincere appreciation to your boss. Even if you don't like them, you can still find one thing sincere and nice to say. Help your boss out every now and then with day-to-day stuff. For example, help them fix their new smartphone settings, or get the directions to some new place they are heading to. This, however, doesn't mean you need to crawl to them.

Ask your boss for their feedback. Find out if there's anything you can do to improve your performance. Give them your honest feedback too when asked for. Don't wait until the next performance review cycle to get this feedback as it may be too late by then to fix any issue.

5. Demonstrate you are "on top" of issues

Acknowledge problems as they occur and show accountability for the performance of your area. This will make your boss more open to listen to you and will help maintain your credibility. Explain issues using simple examples or metaphors and a language that is easy to understand. Don't overload your boss with too many technical details or jargon, for as Albert Einstein once said: "If you can't explain it simply, you don't understand it well enough".

Come up with options and pros and cons for each option to help both you and your boss make an informed decision. Seek the support of your boss when needed, and let them know exactly what input is required from their side.

Prepare a solid plan to remedy the situation (corrective measures) and to stop similar future occurrences (preventive measures). Ensure you tackle the root cause of the problem and account for all important factors (e.g. tasks, resources, people, and timelines). This will convey the message that you have the nuts and bolts of the issue as well as the big-picture perspective.

6. Negotiate your workloads

Always be realistic when it comes to accepting more workloads. Don't over promise, or again your credibility and reputation will be at stake. Explain to your boss the consequences and risks if they overload you. Instead of saying "yes" to everything your boss asks you to do, negotiate. Ask them to re-prioritize your list of tasks, or try to suggest who else could be involved.

7. Keep your boss informed

Make sure your boss isn't caught by surprise, especially in meetings they attend with upper management. Make sure they don't get the information about your area from others too often.

Try to be the good news messenger. This will eventually make your boss build a positive mental association between seeing you and having a pleasant mood. Still if there is bad news, you have to have the courage to share it with your boss so you can work it out together.

8. Build your network

Depending on a single boss might limit your career advancement. Take the time to build a network with other managers at the same level as your boss and also with those at higher levels, especially the ones who have input into your work, who evaluate you or your team, and who you rely on to get your work done.

This network is valuable assets that can help you get the most out of yourself, and can become your gateway to a whole new array of opportunities, knowledge, and experiences. Be sure to build this network with integrity and positive purpose. It's important not to jeopardize the hard work you've put in building a productive relationship with your own boss.

Chapter 11: Learn How To Motivate And Inspire

One day you might assume a supervisory or a managerial role, where you will have to perform and deliver through other people. And, your task then will be to encourage your employees to consistently push their limits and offer their best at work. This proves to be a challenging task, especially if you are leading a team of skilled professionals who have the choice either to stay in your team, or take their knowledge, expertise, and perhaps their networks of relationships and leave. Your task becomes even more challenging when you find yourself stuck between the hammer of your commitment to upper management to tightly control the team's payroll, and the anvil of keeping your team members motivated and loyal to working with you.

So, here comes the popular question that is often asked by people managers and team leaders: "How to get the most out of my employees without paying them extra money?" To answer this question, I will try to combine my own practical observations with the insights of remarkable researchers in the field to show you the five areas that you need to work on. As the below figure suggests, there are three areas that represent the necessary foundation for the success of any motivational effort you may exert, and two areas that are considered as real motivation boosters:

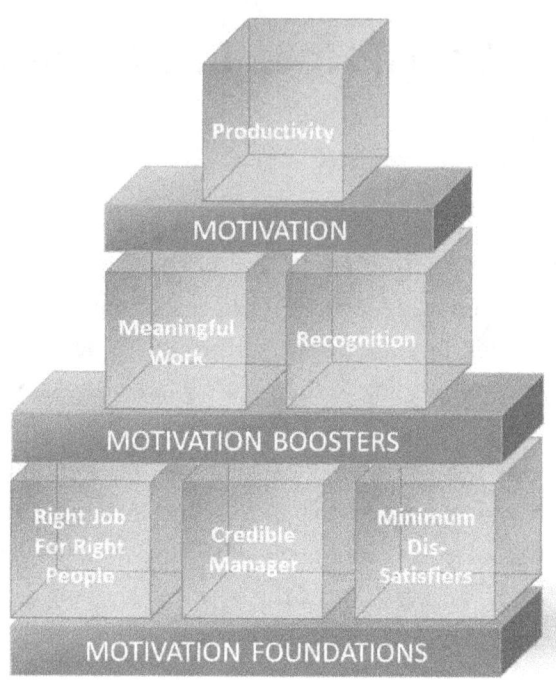

Figure 11.1   The Five Areas of Motivation

1. It all starts with hiring the right people for the right job

It really makes your job motivating your employees much easier if you allow everyone to do what they can do best, and perform the job that matches their skills, qualifications, and natural preferences. In their book "12 The Elements of Great Managing", Rodd Wagner & James K. Harter call this the "sweet spot" of employment. However, managers seldom find enough freedom assigning every team member the kind of job he or she prefers.

Your task is then to innovatively try to craft a role for everybody that is closest to their sweet spot, while working within the given organizational or team constraints. There exist a myriad of management books that discuss the ideas of job rotation, job enlargement (widening the job scope by adding more tasks), and job enrichment (increasing the job depth and giving the employee more autonomy). However, unless your organization is widely committed to the implementation of these practices, you -as an individual manager- have a little to do here.

This is why I suggest you another helpful tool that you can apply more readily to your team to help achieving the needed fit between people and tasks. That is the "Belbin team inventory". Using that tool, you can understand employees' behavioral preferences and accordingly assign them to one of three role types: action oriented roles, people oriented roles, or problem solving roles. You can access this tool at: www.belbin.com

Another key management responsibility on your shoulders is to help a struggling employee. Good people are sometimes placed in the wrong jobs. I've personally seen this happening many times, and it drains the life out of the employee. You need to recognize this and reassign them before they hurt the company or lose their self-confidence. This way they can have the chance to thrive.

2. There is a little that you can do if they don't see you as a "credible" manager

Credibility is a very important foundation for all human relationships including with no doubt your relationship with your subordinates, for without credibility, people will not trust your actions or intentions, and no amount of praise that you may show them will suffice to really make them productive or happy to work for you, simply because they will be busy trying to protect themselves against you!

Your credibility hinges on both your character and your competence. Stephen M.R. Covey and Rebecca R. Merrill offer an impressive framework to understand and build credibility in their book "The Speed of Trust".

Character in that sense is about having integrity and intent. Integrity means doing what you say, saying what you do, committing only to what is consistent with your values, and keeping your promises. Intent has to do with clarifying your intentions, motives, and agendas.

Competence means that you must have the necessary skills and capabilities to perform your role as a manager, and also possess a good record of achievements. There are three types of managerial skills that you need to develop: sufficient knowledge about your business area, problem solving skills, and relationship building skills.

Think of your own boss and see how you would personally react if you perceive that he or she doesn't walk the talk, has a hidden agenda, or is incompetent in his or her role.

3. Keep "dis-satisfiers" at a minimum

"Satisfiers" are factors in the job itself that lead to strong satisfaction and motivation when they are present and lead to dissatisfaction when they are missing. "Dis-satisfiers", on the other hand, are factors in the work atmosphere not in the job itself and they work in one direction only, meaning that they do not lead to a strong satisfaction and motivation when they are present, but do cause a lot of dissatisfaction when they are missing.

It is interesting that we realize now through lots of empirical research that employee salary for example is a "dis-satisfiers" not a "satisfier". Employees will look around to see if they are being compensated fairly with regard to their efforts and in comparison to their peers. If they perceive that they lack appropriate compensation, they will surely be dissatisfied. On the other side, if they see that their pay already equate to their efforts and to that of their peers, then any additional pay raise that you attempt to offer will only make them come happier to work for few days, and then it will be taken for granted.

You also need to keep an eye on and try to neutralize the impact of other "dis-satisfiers" like keeping acceptable and safe physical working conditions, availing the tools and equipment necessary for your employees to carry out their work, and encouraging healthy relationships between team members. The latter is gaining more significance as employees are spending more time than ever at work, and hence are basing more of their personal relationships around work and are even expecting to have best friends at work.

4. Give your employees meaningful work

Employees need to understand clearly what is expected from them. They need to know and have a say in their work objectives and what they are required to do to achieve them. They also need to be taught which behaviors and outcomes constitute a great performance, and how this performance is going to be rewarded and how it affects their career progress.

The higher you realistically expect from your people, the higher they will achieve. Set stretch goals that cover all job aspects. For instance, a sales person's goals need not to focus solely on sales quotas, but to consider also factors like collection efficiency, relationships with clients, coworkers, and other teams, and completeness of documentations. Try to innovatively quantify the difficult-to-measure goals instead of just omitting them all together. The benefit of doing so is that you will orient the team to juggle all work aspects simultaneously while allowing everybody to attain the performance evaluation grade he or she fairly deserves.

You must also create an environment that tolerates authentic mistakes. Those are the inevitable errors that accompany trying something new, which are different of course from the errors that result from careless or irresponsible attitude. This way, people will be encouraged to take calculated risks and have the chance to learn and prosper.

It is vital for people to see how their work connects to the overall organization's mission and performance, and to realize how it affects other operations and teams. The reason is that people try to create meaning for what they do and to frame their activities within a larger purpose, for their own survival and peace of mind. When you help your employees properly establish this sense of purpose, they will not only work harder, but will feel that their work helps identify who they are, and they will eventually go the extra mile to make sure there is nothing that hampers their ability to do a good job. Simply they will become more "engaged".

In the midst of all of this, don't overlook the need to maintain a healthy work-life balance for your people. More organizations are starting to apply schemes like flexible hours, reduced work week, and telecommuting, in order to keep their employees satisfied. Even if you are not in a position to decide your company's human resources policies, you still have enough influence to give your employees chances to take enough leisure times and to take enough care of their own wellbeing and their families.

After all, remember to keep timely and bi-directional communication with your employees. Meet with them at least weekly and listen actively to their ideas and concerns. Give them on-the-spot, honest feedback instead of waiting till the next performance review, as it could be too late by then to fix issues. This way you will save them confusion and frustration.

5. Recognize their achievements

Do you know that 80% of employees who quit their jobs report that they do so mainly because of a lack of appreciation? (This is according to a comprehensive 10 years study by the Jackson organization). That is why best managers know the importance of recognition as a tool to boost their employee morale and motivation and improve their performance. This is also what Adrian Gostick and Chester Elton confirm in their book "The Carrot Principle", where they also mention more than 120 cool recognition ideas.

Sincere and frequent appreciation for employees' achievements and desirable behaviors has a dramatic effect on their performance. The reason is that people sub-consciously develop a mental association between their behavior and its consequences. If their behavior results in a pleasant consequence like praise or recognition, they will love to repeat it in order to gratify themselves with praise and recognition again. Conversely, if their behavior results in an unpleasant consequence, like indifference or even blame they will tend to stop it.

The one very important thing here for you is to understand that employees can easily sense a superficial recognition that is being done merely because managers are told to send the employees "Thank You" letters or hand them out gift certificates, just as a matter of compliance with the company's recognition program, or to keep the employees productive, but without a real interest in them as human beings.

To give sincere recognition, you first need to know your employees well, and then to personalize your recognition and tailor it for each individual employee to suit his or her interests and lifestyle. For example, if an employee is a football maniac, give him a couple of tickets for a championship final.

Don't be reluctant to give recognition just because you fear that it might stimulate jealousy among employees. If you do it objectively and fairly, everybody will have the chance to be recognized for his or her good work. This, however, doesn't mean to make it like a turn for every employee regardless of his or her performance, or again the recognition will lose its significance.

There are lots of free and symbolic recognition ideas at your disposal, starting from a bat on their shoulder and an honest "Thank you", to allowing them to take a vacation during the loaded times, celebrating their achievements, allotting them a corner office, giving them a higher priority for external training, or granting them the opportunity to learn something new at work. Finally, you need to realize that people need to be recognized even for just doing the job they are paid for.

Chapter 12: Move Up Your Career Ladder

A successful career is an important factor for leading a satisfying life, as it helps people actualize themselves and drive a sense of purpose. An unfulfilling career, on the other hand, just resembles a bad personal relationship in which people may get preoccupied to the extent that it becomes a major cause of life stress.

If you feel that you are dead-ended in the wrong job or that your career is only progressing too slow to meet your aspirations, then you share this same feeling with 33% of the workers who were recently surveyed by the Wall Street Journal, and who stay in their jobs only to be able to pay their bills. To find out the reality of your situation and take steps to change it, consider these advices:

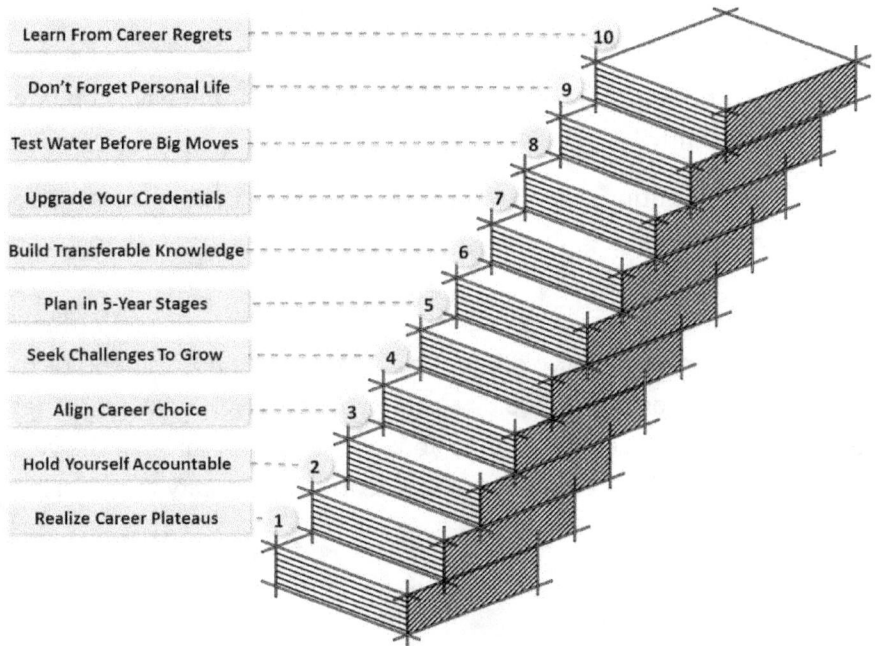

Figure 12.1   The Ten Essentials for Advancing Your Career

1. Realize it when you are trapped in a "career plateau"

A career plateau is the situation in which your career stagnates. Your chances of moving up the career ladder diminish. This could happen because of reasons that have to do with your organization, like the end of advancement or the lack of challenges, or more seriously, it could happen because of personal reasons, like loss of identity, direction, meaning, self-esteem, or when one undergoes self-doubt in his or her life. Ask yourself the below questions to realize whether you are currently trapped in a career plateau:

- Do I accept high-visibility assignments?

- Am I recognized by other leaders in my organization?

- Am I routinely promoted?

- Am I known as a versatile employee?

- Do I continue to get larger-than-normal raises?

- Do I rate at the high end of the performance ratings?

- Do I have a plan with measurable objectives, and have I updated it recently?

- Do I continue to advance my education, both formal and vocational?

If your answer to most of these questions is "No", then you probably are experiencing a career plateau. Don't worry. It is not the end of the line. To escape, or better avoid, a career plateau, you need to recheck or redefine what success means to you, and look back through the years to reassess your early career goals and reaffirm or modify them, in light of your life priorities.

2. Hold yourself accountable for your career success

It all starts here! For without a clear sense of personal accountability about your own career success, you would easily blame any stagnation that you may encounter on bad luck, prejudiced boss, tough economy, or another hundred reasons, but yourself. Highly effective people are found to have an "internal locus of control", which means they believe they are in control of their lives, and that most of the events that happen to them stem basically from their own actions.

The organization or the boss that you work for, might of course play a role in supporting your career progress and skills development, but only to the extent that is necessary to serve their own objectives and performance commitments. At the end, they still have no obligation finding you a rewarding job or a development opportunity that meet your ambitions. It's you, yourself, who are chiefly responsible for shaping your own career path.

3. Align your career choices with your interests and strengths

From the very first chapter of this book, you have come to realize the importance of knowing your interests, motivators, and skills, for you to be able to choose a fulfilling career. To gain this valuable knowledge about yourself, take the various self-assessments at the end of this book. Beside that, Marcus Buckingham in his book "The Truth About You", advises that you spend some time to reflect and to ask yourself: What elements of your work do you love? What would you love to be asked to do? Outside of work, what do you like the most? How do you like to spend you leisure time? What do you like to read? What type of people do you enjoy? Use your answers to pinpoint your primary interests. When you know what you truly love, you will be in a better position to find a satisfying career. Don't settle for anything that doesn't interest you.

Now, is it possible to find a job that perfectly suits you? The answer is probably "No". However, you can still "build" your almost-ideal job brick by brick by focusing on work activities that best play to your interests and strengths. Volunteer for special assignments or give your boss a suggestion about some activity you could handle. At the same time, you need to neutralize your weaknesses by stopping to engage in activities that expose them. This may not always be possible at work, but it is worth trying: you can partner with someone in your organization who has strengths in areas where you have weaknesses. Alternatively, focus more on your strengths to make some of your weaknesses less important.

4. To grow, seek challenge

There is a story about a man who found a cocoon for a butterfly. One day a small opening appeared, he sat and watched the butterfly for several hours as it struggled to force its body through the little hole. Then it seemed to stop making any progress. It appeared stuck. The man decided to help the butterfly and with a pair of scissors he cut open the cocoon. The butterfly then emerged easily. Something was strange. The butterfly had a swollen body and shriveled wings. The man watched the butterfly expecting it to take on its correct proportions. But nothing changed.

The butterfly stayed the same. It was never able to fly. In his kindness and haste the man did not realize that the butterfly's struggle to get through the small opening of the cocoon is nature's way of forcing fluid from the body of the butterfly into its wings so that it would grow and become ready to fly.

Like a butterfly needs to struggle through its cocoon so that it can grow normally and become able to fly, we all need to be challenged through our jobs so that we can learn, develop, and grow in our careers. That is why you must always appreciate, and even seek challenge. Ask for broader job responsibilities, stretch your performance goals, opt in for new, non-routine initiatives, search for lateral moves, or even consider a transfer to another region or office. Disrupt your comfort zone.

5. Plan your career in five- year stages

We live in a more than ever changing environment, which inherently makes it not feasible to look into or plan for the very far future. Try to plan your career in five-year stages, by letting your strategy emerge based on where trends seem to be going, and after all, recognize that you cannot fully determine the trajectory of your career. There are just too many factors beyond your control that will affect your career options: economic trends, political situation, and technological changes, to name a few. Keep an eye on your environment and stay ready for the exceptional window of opportunity to non-linearly advance your professional life.

6. Build "transferable" knowledge

Transferable knowledge is knowledge that you can reuse in a wide variety of sectors and functions. For instance, knowledge about contract negotiations can be quite helpful for sales managers as well as procurement managers in almost any sector. Building such knowledge will then boost your career choices and make you more attractive to employers. Search for the kind of job opportunities that will allow you to build transferable knowledge.

Gaining experience outside your home country is one way to build transferable knowledge, as it will help you learn to deal with different economic, cultural, and political environments. Similarly, you can try working in different types of organizations during your career. Robert C. Bozen, a lecturer of business administration at Harvard Business School stresses that For-profit organizations may be concerned about hiring people who have spent their entire career in government, for instance.

7. Upgrade your credentials

If you know that obtaining a certain credential will make you more competitive and will support your career advancement, just go for it. Don't make excuses about lack of time, as you don't necessarily have to invest in a lengthy degree program. There are alternatives, such as professional certificates. If you are an accountant, you can improve your technical skills with a CPA certificate. If you are a program manager, you may seek an MSP certificate. If you are a quality specialist, go get a Six Sigma green/black belt, and so on. Just do enough research about the most suitable credentials and the awarding institutions before making this investment that will surely pay off. Check this website for certifications:

www.careertech.org/career-clusters/resources/credentials.html

8. Test the water before big moves

To better manage the risks that come with any big career decision, you need to test the water first. If you are an employee who is pondering on starting his own business, you may experiment with it on nights and weekends to see if it can work before quitting your job to make it full-fledged. If you are considering a new offer in a fundamentally new environment (e.g. new country, new culture, or new industry), gather enough information and consider all the consequences of your decision. Always make sure you have a plan B that you can fail-safe to, should your move stumble.

9. Don't forget your personal life, hobbies and passions

Balancing your professional and personal lives is key to your long-term success. This is easier said than done, however, you must strive to achieve it. Good time management will help you better meet your family commitments and spend the time to sharpen your saw, which is, in fact, your body, soul, mind and heart. Pray regularly and exercise at least three times a week, and don't forget to reserve a slot for your hobbies and passions. After all, enjoy what you have.

10. Learn from your career regrets

All people, no matter how successful they are, what roles they assume, or what their line of work is, have regrets about some bad career decisions they have made in the past. Highly successful people only know how to learn from their regrets and turn them into a positive energy for change. The biggest career regrets, as per Daniel Gulati, a blogger of Harvard Business Review, are:

- Taking the job mainly for the money
- Not quitting the old job early enough
- Lacking the confidence to start their own business
- Not acting on career hunches (e.g. declining opportunities that proved later to be very promising

Chapter 13: Do You Want To Become Your Own Boss?

Are you seriously considering starting your own business, pursuing new opportunities and becoming your own boss? If your answer is "Yes", then you share your intention with around one fifth of the world's adult population, who are either actively trying to start a business or already owning and managing a business - according to a recent report on entrepreneurial activity that was issued by the Global Entrepreneurship Monitor (GEM).

But before taking your first steps into that thrilling world, you need first to know the answers to these questions: Who is an "Entrepreneur"? What are his or her qualities? What are the drawbacks that come with entrepreneurial life? What are the deadly mistakes entrepreneurs make? How to avoid them? And, do you have what it takes to become an entrepreneur? This chapter attempts to help you find answers to these questions.

1. Who is the "entrepreneur"?

The classic entrepreneur is a risk-taking individual who takes action to pursue opportunities and situations others may fail to recognize as such, or may even view as problems or threats. The entrepreneur is a one who creates a new business in the face of uncertainty, for achieving profit and growth, and in doing so, they assemble the necessary resources to capitalize on those opportunities.

It's really inspiring to think how some business magnates started their success stories at a very young age and before they even complete their education. Take Richard Branson as an example. He is the founder and chairman of Virgin Group that has more than 400 companies. He is the 4th richest citizen of the United Kingdom. His first business venture was a magazine called "Student" at the age of 16!

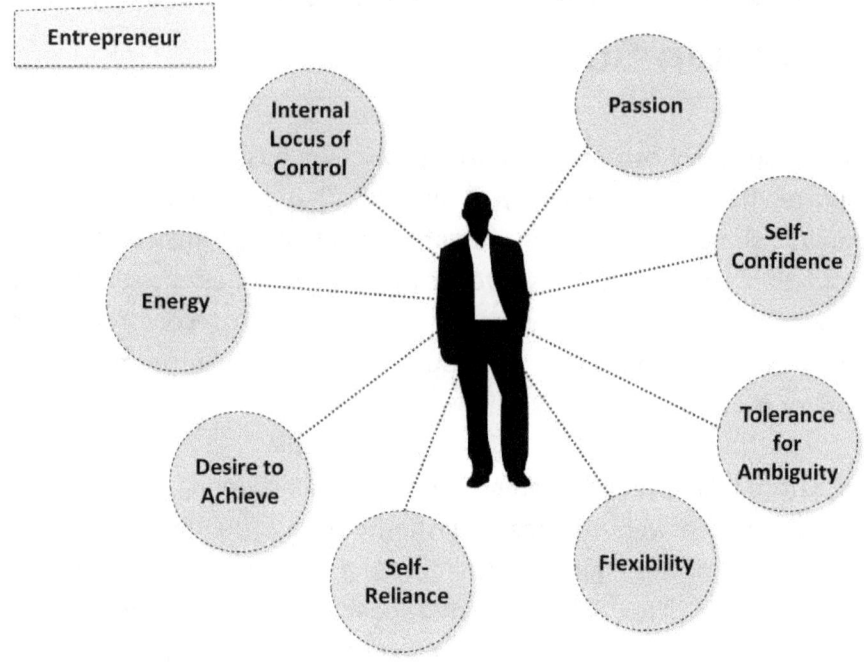

Entrepreneur

Internal Locus of Control

Passion

Energy

Self-Confidence

Desire to Achieve

Tolerance for Ambiguity

Self-Reliance

Flexibility

Figure 13.1   Qualities of an Entrepreneur

2. What are the qualities of an entrepreneur?

Anyone -regardless of age, race, gender, color, national origin, or any other demographic factor- can become an entrepreneur. However, the noted psychologist David McClelland characterizes entrepreneurs as possessing these qualities:

- **Internal locus of control**: entrepreneurs believe that they control their own destiny; they are self-directing and like autonomy.

- **High energy**: entrepreneurs are persistent, hard-working, and willing to exert extraordinary efforts to succeed.

- **Desire for achievement**: entrepreneurs are motivated to act individually to accomplish challenging goals; they thrive on feedback.

- **Tolerance for ambiguity**: entrepreneurs are risk takers; they tolerate situations with high degrees of uncertainty.

- **Self-confidence**: entrepreneurs feel competent, believe in themselves, and are willing to make decisions.

- **Passion and action-orientation**: entrepreneurs try to act ahead of problems; they want to get things done and not to waste valuable time.

- **Self-reliance and desire for independence**: entrepreneurs want to be their own bosses, not to work for others.

- **Flexibility**: entrepreneurs are willing to admit problems and errors, and are willing to change a course of action when plans are not working.

Interestingly enough, it's found that entrepreneurs also tend to have unique backgrounds and life experiences, including:

- **Childhood experiences and family environment**: Entrepreneurs tend to have parents who were entrepreneurs or self-employed. They tend to be raised in families that encourage responsibility, initiative, and independence.

- **Career or work history**: Entrepreneurs often try more than one business venture. They tend to have prior career or personal experience in the business area or industry in which they develop an entrepreneurial activity. Most entrepreneurs start their businesses between the ages of 22 and 45; however, age is no barrier.

- **Deeply embedded life interests**: Entrepreneurs have strong interests in creative production. They seek the sense of mastery that comes with success.

To know if you possess the qualities of a successful entrepreneur, take the self-assessment: <u>Do I Have What It Takes To Become An Entrepreneur?</u> (Pg. 165)

3. What are the drawbacks that come with entrepreneurship?

You are probably aware that entrepreneurs may experience uncertainty of income: "The entrepreneur is the last one to be paid." They risk losing their entire investment, in addition to the long hours and hard work they have to put into their initiatives, coupled with the high levels of stress and discouragement they encounter until the business takes off.

If you are willing to go through all these turbulences during your journey, and are ready to sacrifice your quality of life only to win your trophy and succeed at the end, then you can become a successful entrepreneur.

4. What are the deadly mistakes of entrepreneurs?

Studies have indicated that the below are the most common mistakes that entrepreneurs commit, and that lead new business ventures into failure:

- **Insufficient financing**: not having enough funds to maintain operations while still building the business and gaining access to customers and markets.
- **Lack of experience**: not having sufficient experience about the essentials of business operations including finance, purchasing, selling, and production. Or lack of knowledge about the chosen market or geographical area.

- **Lack of strategic thinking**: not taking the time to find the propitious niche to serve efficiently or to determine what unique proposition will be offered to the customers.

- **Poor financial control**: not keeping track of the numbers, and failure to control business finances and use existing monies to best advantage.

- **Growing too fast**: not taking the time to consolidate a position, fine-tune the organization, and systematically meet the challenges of growth.

- **Lack of commitment**: not devoting enough time to the requirements of running a competitive business.

- **Ethical failure**: falling prey to the temptations of fraud, deception, and embezzlement.

5. How to avoid these mistakes?

Entrepreneurs can increase their chances for success if they:

- Know their business in depth.

- Develop a solid business plan in writing that describes all the details necessary to set the direction for the new business and to obtain the necessary financing to operate it.

- Efficiently manage their financial resources and understand the financial statements.

- Learn to manage people effectively.

- Conduct sufficient market research to set their offerings apart from those of competition.

- Maintain a positive attitude.

Chapter 14: Control Your Stress

Modern day stress seems to be more widespread than ever and many of the reasons are obvious, such as more work by less people, financial uncertainty, job insecurity, constant performance measurement, the increasing requirement for instant information or response, impossible targets, juggling work/home priorities, the downsides of cyberspace technology, the depressing state of affairs in many parts of the world, among many other things.

Stress can have detrimental effects on our minds and bodies if left unhandled. And, sometimes we are stressed but are not even aware of it, or refuse to admit it and try to hide it from others. In both cases, it might escalate and become more harmful. This chapter will try to portray the nature of stress, its causes and signs, and suggest to you different strategies to cope with it.

1. Understand stress

Ask different people what stress is for them, and you might be surprised with the vast amount of definitions you'll get. Some of their thoughts about stress will probably be: being made to feel insignificant, trying to please everyone all the time, horrible tight feeling in the chest, having no time for oneself, fear of failure, not acting naturally most of the time, or when trivial things seem very important. Apparently, it is a highly relative and personal subject that centers more on feelings than on facts.

However, to better understand stress and learn how to manage it, we need a more uniform and concrete definition. Researchers define stress as a reaction to excessive pressure, or demand (stressor, real or perceived) which seems difficult or impossible to manage. Or simply, like David Newth defines it in his book "Stress and Work/Life Balance", stress is the feeling of instability due to losing control. These definitions carry the clear implication of our choice both of how we interpret the causes of stress, and our judgment about managing stress.

- **Signs of stress**: The first step to manage anything is to become aware it exists. Stressors, however, are sometimes illusive and may not be well recognized on a conscious level. So, identifying the various physical, emotional, and behavioral signs of stress may help alert you when you are suffering stress:

- Physical signs: palpitations - throbbing heart, pain and tightness in the chest, indigestion, breathlessness, nausea, muscle twitches, tiredness, headache, vague aches or pains, skin irritation or rashes, susceptibility to allergies, clenched fists or jaw, feeling faint, frequent colds, flu or other infections, recurrence of previous illnesses, constipation or diarrhea, rapid weight gain or loss, and alteration of the menstrual pattern in women.

- Emotional signs: swings in mood, increased worrying, feeling tense, drained, no enthusiasm, feeling angry, guilty, cynical, feeling nervous, apprehensive, anxious, feelings of helplessness, loss of confidence and self-esteem, and lack of concentration, withdrawal into day-dreams.

- Behavioral signs: proneness to accidents, poor work, increased dependence on nicotine, alcohol or drugs, overeating or loss of appetite, change in sleep pattern, difficulty in getting to sleep and waking tired, loss of interest in sex, impaired speech, withdrawal from supportive relationships, irritability, taking work home more, too busy to relax, not looking after oneself, and speeding up - talking, walking, eating, drinking.

- **Types of stressors**: It's valuable to distinguish among three types of stressors: life-changing stressors, chronic stressors, and non-event stressors, for the amount of influence that you can exert over the stressor, and the most suitable coping strategy will differ from one type to another:

- Life-Changing Events: discrete events that require some social and/or psychological adjustment on your part. They can be recent (within the past year), or remote (childhood events). They can be negative events (like divorce, death of a close family member, or being fired from job), as well as positive events (like marriage, a promotion, or inheritance). Life-changing events can build up and create stress. If they accumulate too much, they can overtake your ability to cope. Some events are uncontrollable by you. Others, however, are within your control. So, the advice here is: Don't try to undertake too much change too fast. The Social Readjustment Rating Scale (SRRS) is an interesting tool that could help you assess your likelihood to suffer stress-induced illnesses or injuries during the next two years, based on events you've encountered in the past year. You may Google that tool and find it freely available on many websites.

- Chronic stressors: events encountered in everyday life, like daily hassles (e.g. waiting in a long queues, getting stuck in traffic), playing multiple life roles at the same time (e.g. parenting, working, being in a relationship), community-wide strains (e.g. living in a high-crime neighborhood, discriminatory behavior due to race, ethnicity, etc.), or persistent life difficulties (e.g. long-term disabilities).

- Non-Event Stressors: desired or anticipated events, when they do not occur (e.g. wanting to graduate but not enough credits, wanting to have an intimate friend of opposite sex as a college student, wanting to get pregnant).

- Stress in the workplace: Stress in the workplace is a major aspect of the topic as many elements of the workplace environment can easily turn into chronic stressors, which is a commonality throughout the world in every business. Managing that stress becomes vital for you to keep up job performance as well as relationships with co-workers and employers. For some workers, changing the work environment relieves work stress. Having less competition between employees decreases some amounts of stress. However, each person is different, and in order to manage stress in the workplace, you will find that employers try to provide stress management programs such as therapy, communication programs, and more flexible work schedules.

- **Burnout**: The way you deal with pressure determines how much stress you feel. If stressors are left unhandled long enough, they lead to physical and emotional collapse, which is known as "burnout". People who suffer burnout feel exhaustion, lack of enthusiasm, indifference, frustration, poor self-image, and/or negative emotions. At work, burnout may occur as a result of a mismatch between the individual and the job, excessive workloads, impossible tasks, a tough boss, difficult clients, or conflicting demands.

Reasons of Job Burnout:

- Mismatch Between Individual And Job
- Excessive Workload
- Impossible Tasks
- Tough Boss
- Difficult Clients
- Conflicting Demands

Figure 14.1   Possible Reasons for Job Burnout

One individual can experience few stressors, but be unable to handle the pressure well and thus eventually falls a victim of burnout. Another person can experience a far greater number or intensity of stressors, but effectively deal with them, and avoid burnout. To learn more about your own proneness to stress and burnout, take the self-assessment: What's My Tendency To Suffer Stress? (Pg. 168). The question now is how can you properly handle and cope with pressures, so as to protect yourself from the negative consequences of stress?

2. Learn how to "cope" with stress

Coping is the ability to deal with stressors and overcome personal and interpersonal problems and difficulties encountered in life. Everyone can actually learn to develop their coping skills. There are basically two types of coping: problem-focused coping, which attempts to alter the situation, or the environment that is causing stress, and emotion-focused coping, which focuses inward and attempts to alter the way one thinks or feels about the situation.

Examples of strategies of problem-focused coping are:

- Time management
- Realistic goal-setting
- Advice-seeking
- Interpersonal conflict resolution
- Utilization of problem solving skills

Examples of strategies of emotion-focused coping are:

- Relaxation
- Physical exercise
- Meditation

- Support groups

If you acknowledge and accept the fact that you are responsible for your stress levels and for the ways you respond to stressful situations, it will actually give you a great deal of power. Once you assume accountability for your own stress, you will gain access to vast number of ways to combat it.

Appendix (A): Self-Assessment Battery

What Are My Career Interests?

Instructions:

Below are two sections of questions about: 1) activities that you as a person can do, and 2) actions that you like to do. In each section, mark only the items that most fit you.

		Can You...			
1	☐	fix electrical things	16	☐	lead a group discussion
2	☐	solve math problems	17	☐	give talks or speeches
3	☐	sketch, draw, paint	18	☐	keep accurate records
4	☐	teach/train others	19	☐	plant a garden
5	☐	initiate projects	20	☐	use a microscope
6	☐	work well within a system	21	☐	sing, act, dance
7	☐	pitch a tent	22	☐	mediate disputes
8	☐	understand scientific theories	23	☐	lead a group
9	☐	play a musical instrument	24	☐	use a computer terminal
10	☐	express yourself clearly	25	☐	operate tools and machine
11	☐	sell things	26	☐	interpret formulas
12	☐	do a lot of paper work in a short time	27	☐	design fashions or interiors
13	☐	play a sport	28	☐	cooperate well with others
14	☐	do complex calculations	29	☐	persuade others

| 15 | ☐ | write stories, poetry, music | 30 | ☐ | write effective business letters |

Do You Like To…					
31	☐	tinker with machines/vehicles	46	☐	do volunteer work
32	☐	explore a variety of ideas	47	☐	start your own business
33	☐	attend concerts, theatre, art exhibits	48	☐	collect or organize things
34	☐	work in groups	49	☐	use your hands
35	☐	make decisions	50	☐	deal with abstractions
36	☐	work with numbers	51	☐	take photography
37	☐	be physically active	52	☐	work with young people
38	☐	work independently	53	☐	meet important people
39	☐	read fiction, plays, and poetry	54	☐	follow clearly defined procedures
40	☐	help people with problems	55	☐	build things
41	☐	be elected to office	56	☐	do research
42	☐	be responsible for details	57	☐	express yourself creatively
43	☐	work outdoors	58	☐	serve others
44	☐	perform lab experiments	59	☐	campaign politically
45	☐	work on crafts	60	☐	type or take shorthand

Score your results as follows: Count one point for each item listed under the six categories in the below table, according to the item numbers you have marked above. For example, if you marked item no. 46, then you count one point under the category "S", and so on.

Score for "R"	Score for "I"	Score for "A"	Score for "S"	Score for "E"	Score for "C"
1	2	3	4	5	6
7	8	9	10	11	12
13	14	15	16	17	18
19	20	21	22	23	24
25	26	27	28	29	30
31	32	33	34	35	36
37	38	39	40	41	42
43	44	45	46	47	48
49	50	51	52	53	54
55	56	57	58	59	60
___	___	___	___	___	___

Now, rank the six categories in a descending order. For example, if your scores are: R=1, I=0, A=10, S=7, E=12, C=3, then your categories will be ordered like that: "EASCRI".

Interpretation:

This questionnaire helps you identify your best career and education choices, by first measuring your interests against six broad categories or themes (described below), and then suggesting the work and education possibilities that best fit your interests. The six themes are:

Realistic (Doers): People who have athletic ability, prefer to work with objects, machines, tools, plants or animals, or to be outdoors.

Investigative (Thinkers): People who like to observe, learn, investigate, analyze, evaluate, or solve problems.

Artistic (Creators): People who have artistic, innovating, or intuitional abilities and like to work in unstructured situations using their imagination and creativity.

Social (Helpers): People who like to work with people to enlighten, inform, help, train, or cure them, or are skilled with words.

Enterprising (Persuaders): People who like to work with people, influencing, persuading, leading or managing for organizational goals or economic gain.

Conventional (Organizers): People who like to work with data, have clerical or numerical ability, carry out tasks in detail, or follow through on others' instructions.

After ranking the six themes, identify your top three, and check what career and education options best match them from the below list:

	Job	Education (Major)
Realistic	Air Traffic Controller, Archaeologist, Athletic Trainer, Cartographer, Commercial Airline Pilot, Farm Manager, Geodetic Surveyor, Laboratory Technician, Landscape Architect, Mechanical Engineer, Optician,	Agriculture, Computer Science (hardware), Earth Science, Engineering, Environmental/ Occupational Health, Forestry, Geography, Geology, Health Science/Nursing, Kinesiology, Leisure

	Petroleum Geologist, Police Officer, Property Manager, Recreation Manager, Service Manager, Surgeon	Studies & Recreation, Physical Therapy, Physics, Veterinary Science
Investigative	Actuary, Biochemist, Biologist, Chemical Engineer, Computer Systems Analyst, Dentist, Ecologist, Economist, Electrical Engineer, Geologist, Mathematician, Meteorologist, Pharmacist, Physician, Programmer, Psychologist, Research Analyst, Statistician, Technical Writer, Veterinarian	Hard Sciences, Medicine, Chemistry, Computer Science, Economics, Engineering, Health Sciences, History, Math, Philosophy, Physics, Psychology, Religious Studies, Social Sciences
Artistic	Actor, Advertising Manager, Architect, Art Teacher, Artist, Copy Writer, Dance Instructor, Drama Coach, Entertainer/Performer, Fashion Illustrator, Film Editor, Interior Designer, Journalist/Reporter, Librarian, Medical Illustrator, Museum Curator, Photographer, Writer, Graphic Designer	Art (all options), Business Communication, Fashion Design, Interior Design, Journalism, Languages, Marketing, Music, Philosophy, Radio-TV-Film, Religious Studies, Speech, Theatre
Social	City Manager, Consumer Affairs Manager, Counselor/Therapist, Historian, Hospital Administrator, Psychologist, Insurance Claims Examiner,	Anthropology, Child Development, Deaf Studies, Family Environ. Sci., Linguistics, Political Science, Psychology, Social Work, Sociology, Teaching, Urban Studies, Women's

	Librarian, Medical Assistant, Minister/Priest/Rabbi, Nurse, Police Officer, Real Estate Appraiser, Preschool Teacher, Recreation Manager, Teacher, Social Worker,	Studies
Enterprising	Advertising Manager, Banker/Financial Planner, Branch Manager, Business Manager, Chamber of Commerce Exec, Credit Analyst, Customer Service Manager, Education & Training Manager, Entrepreneur, Insurance Manager, Lawyer/Attorney, Office Manager, Personnel Recruiter, Politician, Public Relations Rep, Sales Manager, Sales Manager, Stockbroker	Business (all options), Communication, Consumer Affairs, Economics, Ethnic Studies, History, Journalism, Law, Political Science, Radio-TV-Film, Sociology, Speech, Urban Studies
Conventional	Accountant, Administrative Assistant, Bank Teller, Budget Analyst, Business Manager, Claims Adjuster, Computer Operator, Court Reporter, Credit Manager, Customs Inspector, Editorial Assistant, Elementary School Teacher, Internal Auditor, Museum Registrar, Payroll Specialist, Safety Inspector, Travel Agent	Accounting, Computer Technology, Counseling, Finance, Health Care, Mgmt. Info. Systems, Office Systems, Real Estate, Teaching, Word Processing

What Motivates Me At Work?

Instructions:

For each of the below statements, rate how true it is for you using the following four-point scale. Try to respond as honestly as you can and work quickly:

		Never True For Me	Occasionally True For Me	Often True For Me	Always True For Me
1	I want to be really good at my job, one of the best, an expert.				
2	I really feel most satisfied when I am able to manage the work of others to achieve a common goal.				
3	Ideally I want to do things my way and to my own timetable.				
4	I would much rather build my own business than being the boss in someone else's.				
5	I believe that security and stability are much more important than having the freedom to choose how I work.				
6	My ideal career will enable me to integrate all of my needs – whether work, personal or family.				

7	It is important to me that I use my talents to further the greater good.				
8	I get a kick out of solving the unsolvable or winning against the odds.				
9	I will only feel really successful when I have the freedom to define my work.				
10	I feel most satisfied and fulfilled when I am able to use my expertise, talents and skills.				
11	I would really like to start my own business one day.				
12	I would be very uncomfortable working in an organization that took a lot of risks. I prefer to work for an organization that offers stability and security.				
13	I would rather seek employment elsewhere than move to a role that seriously undermined my ability to serve the greater good/others.				
14	I prefer to work on projects that really challenge my problem solving skills and have a competitive element.				
15	I would rather find a new job than accept a role that puts constraints on how I do my work.				

16	Balancing my work with my family and personal commitments is more important to me than a senior position.				
17	One day I would like to be the boss, in charge of a whole organization.				
18	Reaching a position of seniority in my area of expertise is far more important to me than becoming a more senior general manager.				
19	I want to make a difference in my career. I will only be truly satisfied if I feel I have made a real contribution to society.				
20	Working on difficult problems is more important to me than achieving a high-level position.				
21	My preference in choosing a role would be to seek out opportunities that minimize any interference with my personal life (family, friends, etc.)				
22	I would feel really fulfilled if I was able to create an enterprise that was primarily the result of my ingenuity, skills and efforts.				
23	Job security and financial independence are really important to me.				
24	I would rather become a general manager with broader responsibilities than become a senior functional manager in my area of expertise.				

This questionnaire taps into the eight career motivators for people:

Technical/functional competence (items 1, 10, and 18)
Power/general management competence (items 2, 17, and 24)
Autonomy/independence (items 3, 9, and 15)
Security/Stability (items 5, 12, and 23)
Entrepreneurial creativity (items 4, 11, and 22)
Service/dedication to a cause (items 7, 13, and 19)
Pure challenge (items 8, 14, and 20)
Lifestyle (items 6, 16, and 21)

Score your response to each question as follows:

"Never True For Me" = 1
"Occasionally True For Me" = 2
"Often True For Me" = 3
"Always True For Me" = 4

Your score on each motivator will vary between 3 and 12. The higher a motivator's score, the more powerful that motivator is for you. Determine your top three motivators.

Interpretation:

We know that we are all very different and are motivated by different things. This questionnaire measures the eight motivators that influence people's career choices. These are defined as follows:

- **Technical/functional competence**: This kind of person likes being good at something and will work to become a guru or expert. They will commit themselves to specializing in their field. They like to be challenged and then use their skill to meet the challenge, doing the job properly and better than almost anyone else. They may be willing to be 'functional managers' but will not value the concerns of general management. If the work does not test their abilities and skills, they will very quickly become bored.

- **Power/general management competence**: Unlike technical/functional people, these individuals want to be managers; and not just to climb the ladder, or earn more money. They find that it is management per se that interests them. They like problem-solving and dealing with other people. They thrive on responsibility and ideally will look to rise up through the organizational levels so they can be in a position to make major policy decisions. To be successful, they will need analytical, emotional, interpersonal and intergroup competence.

- **Autonomy/independence**: Some people come to recognize that they find it really hard to be bound by other people's rules, procedures, working hours, or dress codes, in short, all of the things that come with working in any kind of organization. Primarily, these people have a need to work under their own rules and steam. Regardless of the type of work, they want to do things in their own way and at their own pace. They like clearly delineated, time-bound work within their area of expertise. As such, they will often gravitate towards careers that afford them as much autonomy as possible.

- **Security/Stability**: Security-focused people seek stability and continuity as a primary factor of their lives. We all need varying degrees of security at different points in our lives, however for some this is the predominant orientation throughout their lives and will certainly guide their career decisions. They will often seek out stable organizations that provide the greatest opportunity for job security. They also tend to prefer stable, predictable work tasks. They also need to believe that loyalty makes a real contribution to an organization's performance.

- **Entrepreneurial creativity**: People who have this anchor, have an overriding need to create new products or services. Whilst creativity exists in one form or another in all the groups, for the entrepreneur creating a new venture, product or service of some sort is essential to their sense of success and fulfillment. They are obsessed with their need to create, are restless and continually require new creative challenges. They like to run their own businesses, but differ from those who seek autonomy in that they will share the workload. Ownership is more important than making money, although this is viewed as a key measure of success.

- **Service/dedication to a cause**: Some people will pursue a career because they want to embody their core values in their work and careers. As such, they have a keener orientation towards their values than any talents or competencies. Their choices will be based on a desire to improve the world in some way. They will want work that allows them to influence their employing organizations in the direction of their values. Service-oriented people are driven by how they can help other people more than using their talents (which may fall in other areas).

- **Pure challenge**: Some people are driven by challenge. They will define success as overcoming tremendous obstacles, solving the unsolvable or winning out against impossible odds. They will seek constant stimulation and difficult problems that they can tackle. Most people will want a degree of challenge in their work, but for this type the challenge is the only thing that matters. Such people will change jobs when the current one gets boring and their career histories can be very varied.

- **Lifestyle**: Initially it appears that the notion that one's career anchor is organized around lifestyle is a contradiction in terms. However, many people who are highly motivated towards a meaningful career find themselves in situations that mean their careers must be integrated into their total lifestyle. This is an evolving process, ergo people who find themselves in this situation want flexibility above all else. When seeking employment they are more likely to be interested in an organization's attitude towards personal/family concerns, than the sector or area of expertise. They may even take long periods off work in which to indulge in their passions.

Understanding the motivators that drive you can help you select a job and a work environment, or make career moves that align with those motivators, and hence you become more satisfied and productive. It's advisable that you have some occupational experience to gain deeper understanding of your motivators, values, and talents.

What Are My Skills?

Instructions:

Instructions:

The tables below contain six groups of skills useful in various occupations. Select as many skills as you have from one or more of the six skill groups:

		Basic Skills
1	☐	Active Learning: Understanding the implications of new information for both current and future problem-solving and decision-making
2	☐	Active Listening: Giving full attention to what other people are saying, taking time to understand the points being made, asking questions as appropriate, and not interrupting at inappropriate times
3	☐	Critical Thinking: Using logic and reasoning to identify the strengths and weaknesses of alternative solutions, conclusions or approaches to problems.
4	☐	Learning Strategies: Selecting and using training/instructional methods and procedures appropriate for the situation when learning or teaching new things
5	☐	Mathematics: Using mathematics to solve problems
6	☐	Monitoring: Monitoring/Assessing performance of yourself, other individuals, or organizations to make improvements or take corrective action
7	☐	Reading Comprehension: Understanding written sentences and paragraphs in work related documents

8	☐	Science: Using scientific rules and methods to solve problems
9	☐	Speaking: Talking to others to convey information effectively
10	☐	Writing: Communicating effectively in writing as appropriate for the needs of the audience

Social Skills		
1	☐	Coordination: Adjusting actions in relation to others' actions
2	☐	Instructing: Teaching others how to do something
3	☐	Negotiation: Bringing others together and trying to reconcile differences
4	☐	Persuasion: Persuading others to change their minds or behavior
5	☐	Service Orientation: Actively looking for ways to help people

6	☐	<u>Social Perceptiveness</u>: Being aware of others' reactions and understanding why they react as they do

Complex Problem Solving Skills		
1	☐	<u>Complex Problem Solving</u>: Identifying complex problems and reviewing related information to develop and evaluate options and implement solutions

Systems Skills		
1	☐	<u>Judgment and Decision Making</u>: Considering the relative costs and benefits of potential actions to choose the most appropriate one
2	☐	<u>Systems Analysis</u>: Determining how a system should work and how changes in conditions, operations, and the environment will affect outcomes
3	☐	<u>Systems Evaluation</u>: Identifying measures or indicators of system performance and the actions needed to improve or correct performance, relative to the goals of the system

Resource Management Skills		
1	☐	<u>Management of Financial Resources</u>: Determining how money will be spent to get the work done, and accounting for these expenditures
2	☐	<u>Management of Material Resources</u>: Obtaining and seeing to the appropriate use of equipment, facilities, and materials needed to do certain work

3	☐	**Management of Personnel Resources**: Motivating, developing, and directing people as they work, identifying the best people for the job
4	☐	**Time Management**: Managing one's own time and the time of others

Technical Skills		
1	☐	**Equipment Maintenance**: Performing routine maintenance on equipment and determining when and what kind of maintenance is needed
2	☐	**Equipment Selection**: Determining the kind of tools and equipment needed to do a job
3	☐	**Installation**: Installing equipment, machines, wiring, or programs to meet specifications
4	☐	**Operation and Control**: Controlling operations of equipment or systems
5	☐	**Operation Monitoring**: Watching gauges, dials, or other indicators to make sure a machine is working properly
6	☐	**Operations Analysis**: Analyzing needs and product requirements to create a design

7	☐	Programming: Writing computer programs for various purposes
8	☐	Quality Control Analysis: Conducting tests and inspections of products, services, or processes to evaluate quality or performance
9	☐	Repairing: Fixing machines or systems using the needed tools
10	☐	Technology Design: Generating or adapting equipment and technology to serve user needs
11	☐	Troubleshooting: Determining causes of operating errors and deciding what to do about it

Score:

There is no particular scoring for this self-assessment. Try to determine your top three skills.

Interpretation:

The skills you have selected represent your skill profile. You can use this profile to look for occupations that match your skills, or know the skills you need to acquire before joining a particular occupation. O*NET OnLine is the largest occupational information network, and it contains - among other things- a database of the skill profiles for more than 970 occupations. Visit the skill search section of O*NET on: http://www.onetonline.org/skills/ to benchmark your skills against those required by different occupations.

What's My Personality Type?

Instructions:

For each statement below, select either option "a" or "b". If you feel both "a" and "b" are true, decide which one is more like you, even if it is only slightly more true.

1. I would rather
a. Solve a new and complicated problem.
b. Work on something I have done before.

2. I like to
a. Work alone in a quiet place.
b. Be where the action is.

3. I want a boss who
a. Establishes and applies criteria in decisions.
b. Considers individual needs and makes exceptions.

4. When I work on a project, I
a. Like to finish it and get some closure.
b. Often leave it open for possible changes.

5. When making a decision, the most important considerations are
a. Rational thoughts, ideas, and data.
b. People's feelings and values.

6. On a project, I tend to
a. Think it over and over before deciding how to proceed.
b. Start working on it right away, thinking about it as I go along.

7. When working on a project, I
a. Maintain as much control as possible.
b. Explore various options.

8. In my work, I prefer to
a. Work on several projects at a time, and learn as much as possible about each one.
b. Have one project that is challenging and keeps me busy.

9. I often
a. Make lists and plans whenever I start something and may hate to seriously alter my plans.
b. Avoid plans and just let things progress as I work on them.

10. When discussing a problem with colleagues, it is easy for me to
a. See "the big picture."
b. Grasp the specifics of the situation.

11. When the phone rings in my office or at home, I usually
a. Consider it an interruption.
b. Do not mind answering it.

12. Which word describes you better?
a. Analytical.
b. Empathetic.

13. When I am working on an assignment, I tend to
a. Work steadily and consistently.
b. Work in bursts of energy with "down time" in between.

14. When I listen to someone talk on a subject, I usually try to
a. Relate it to my own experience and see if it fits.
b. Assess and analyze the message.

15. When I come up with new ideas, I generally
a. "Go for it."
b. Like to contemplate the ideas some more

16. When working on a project, I prefer to
a. Narrow the scope so it is clearly defined.
b. Broaden the scope to include related aspects.

17. When I read something, I usually
a. Confine my thoughts to what is written there.
b. Read between the lines and relate the words to other ideas.

18. When I have to make a decision in a hurry, I often
a. Feel uncomfortable and wish I had more information.
b. Am able to do so with available data.

19. In a meeting, I tend to
a. Continue formulating my ideas as I talk about them.
b. Only speak out after I have carefully thought the issue through.

20. In work, I prefer spending a great deal of time on issues of
a. Ideas.
b. People.

21. In meetings, I am most often annoyed with people who
a. Come up with many sketchy ideas.
b. Lengthen meetings with many practical details.

22. I am a
a. Morning person.
b. Night owl.

23. What is your style in preparing for a meeting?
a. I am willing to go in and be responsive.
b. I like to be fully prepared and usually sketch an outline of the meeting.

24. In a meeting, I would prefer for people to
a. Display a fuller range of emotions.
b. Be more task oriented.

25. I would rather work for an organization where
a. My job was intellectually stimulating.
b. I was committed to its goals and mission.

26. On weekends, I tend to
a. Plan what I will do.
b. Just see what happens and decide as I go along.

27. I am more
a. Outgoing.
b. Contemplative.

28. I would rather work for a boss who is
a. Full of new ideas.
b. Practical

In the following, choose the word in each pair that appeals to you more:

29. a. Social.
   b. Theoretical.

30. a. Ingenuity.
   b. Practicality.

31. a. Organized.
   b. Adaptable.

32. a. Active.
   b. Concentration.

Score:

Score your results as follows: Count one point for each statement option listed under the categories in the below tables, according to your responses above. For example, if you chose option "a" for statement no.1, then you count one point under the category "S", but if you chose option "b" for the same statement, then you count one point under the category "N", and so on.

Score for "I"	Score for "E"	Score for "S"	Score for "N"
2a	2b	1a	1b
6a	6b	10b	10a
11a	11b	13a	13b
15b	15a	16a	16b
19b	19a	17a	17b
22a	22b	21a	21b
27b	27a	28b	28a
32b	32a	30b	30a

Total

Identify the one with the more points: I or E	Identify the one with the more points: S or N

Score for "T"	Score for "F"	Score for "J"	Score for "P"
3a	3b	4a	4b
5a	5b	7a	7b
12a	12b	8b	8a
14b	14a	9a	9b
20a	20b	18b	18a

24b	24a	23b	23a
25a	25b	26a	26b
29b	29a	31a	31b

Total

Identify the one with
the more points: T or
F

Identify the one with
the more points: J or
P

Now combine your score into a four-letter personality classification. For example: "ISTJ"

Interpretation:

This questionnaire classifies people's personalities according to four dimensions:

Extroverted or **I**ntroverted (E or I): the way we interact with the world
Sensing or **I**ntuitive (S or N): the way we gather information
Thinking or **F**eeling (T or F): the way we make decisions
Perceiving or **J**udging (P or J): the way we organize and structure our lives

These classifications can then be combined into 16 personality types (for example, INTJ, ENTP). Find your personality, interpretation, and possible career choices* from the following:

ISTJ: You're organized, compulsive, private, trustworthy, and practical. Possible careers are where you can use your experiences and attention to detail to get the task done (e.g. management, administration law enforcement, accounting).

ISFJ: You're loyal, amiable, and willing to make sacrifices for the greater good. Possible careers are where you can draw on your base experience to personally help people in a behind-the-scenes manner (e.g. education, health care, religious settings).

INFJ: You're reflective, introspective, creative, and contemplative. Possible careers are where you can facilitate emotional, intellectual, or spiritual development (e.g. religion, counseling, teaching, arts).

INTJ: You're skeptical, critical, independent, determined, and often stubborn. Possible careers are where you can use your intellectual creativity and technical knowledge to conceptualize, analyze, and get the task done (e.g. scientific or technical fields, computers, law).

ISTP: You're observant, cool, unpretentious, and highly pragmatic. Possible careers are where you can use your hands-on, analytical work with data or things (e.g. skilled trades, technical fields, agriculture, law enforcement, military).

ISFP: You're warm, sensitive, unassuming, and artistic. Possible careers are where you can use your gentle, service-related attentiveness to detail (e.g. health care, business, law enforcement).

INFP: You're reserved, creative, and highly idealistic. Possible careers are where you can use your creativity and focus on your values (e.g. counseling, writing, arts).

INTP: You're socially cautious, enjoy problem solving, and highly conceptual. Possible careers are where you can use your solitary, objective analysis of problems based on your technical expertise (e.g. scientific or technical fields).

ESTP: You're outgoing, live for the moment, unconventional, and spontaneous. Possible careers are where you can use your action-oriented focus to attend to the necessary details (e.g. marketing, skilled trades, business, law enforcement, applied technology).

ESFP: You're sociable, fun-loving, spontaneous, and very generous. Possible careers are where you can use your outgoing nature and enthusiasm to help people with their practical needs (e.g. health care, teaching, coaching, childcare worker, skilled trades).

ENFP: You're people-oriented, creative, and highly optimistic. Possible careers are where you can use creativity and communication to foster the growth of others (e.g. counseling, teaching, religion, arts).

ENTP: You're innovative, individualistic, versatile, and entrepreneurial. Possible careers are where you have the opportunity to take on new challenges continually (e.g. science, management, technology, arts).

ESTJ: You're realistic, logical, analytical, decisive, and have a natural head for business or mechanics. You like to organize and run things. Possible careers are where you can use logic and organization of the facts to get the task done (management, administration, law enforcement).

ESFJ: You're gracious, have good interpersonal skills, and are eager to please. Possible careers are where you can use your personal concern to provide services to others (e.g. education, health care, religion).

ENFJ: You're charismatic, compassionate, and highly persuasive. Possible careers are where you can help others with their emotional, intellectual, and spiritual growth (e.g. religions, arts, teaching).

ENTJ: You're outgoing, visionary, and argumentative, have a low tolerance for incompetence, and often seen as a natural leader. Possible careers are where you can use tough-minded analysis, strategic planning, and organization to get the task done (e.g. management, leadership).

What's My Emotional Intelligence?

Instructions:

For each item below, rate how frequently you demonstrate the ability described. Before responding, try to think of actual situations in which you have been called on to use the ability. Rate each item on the following five-point scale:

		Almost Never	Seldom	Some times	Usually	Almost Always
1	I am aware–from moment to moment–of my feelings as they change.					
2	I act before I think.					
3	When I want something, I can resist the temptation to have it now if that will bring me a greater reward later on					
4	I bounce back quickly from life's setbacks					
5	I can pick up subtle social cues that indicate others' needs or wants.					
6	I'm very good at handling myself in social situations.					

7	I'm persistent in going after the things I want.					
8	When people share their problems with me, I'm good at putting myself in their shoes.					
9	When I'm in a bad mood, I make a strong effort to get out of it.					
10	I can find common ground and build rapport with people from all walks of life.					

Score:

This questionnaire taps into the five basic dimensions of EI: self-awareness (items 1 and 9), self-management (2 and 4), self-motivation (3 and 7), empathy (5 and 8), and social skills (6 and 10). Score your response to each question as follows:

"Almost Never" = 1
"Seldom" = 2
"Sometimes" = 3
"Usually" = 4
"Almost Always" = 5

Your overall score will fall between 10 and 50. While no definite cutoff scores are available, scores of 40 or higher indicate a high EI. Scores of 20 or less suggest a relatively low EI.

Interpretation:

Emotional intelligence (EI) is an assortment of skills and competencies that have shown to influence a person's ability to succeed in coping with environmental demands and pressures. People with high EI have the ability to accurately perceive, evaluate, express, and regulate emotions and feelings.

EI may be most predictive of performance in jobs such as sales or management where success is as dependent on interpersonal skills as technical ability. EI should also be relevant in selecting members to teams. People with low EI are likely to have difficulty managing others, making effective sales presentations, and working on teams.

What's My Communication Style?

Instructions:

Complete the following questionnaire. Rate each statement on the following five-point scale:

		Strongly Disagree	Disagree	Neutral	Agree	Strongly Agree
1	I readily express admiration for others.					
2	What I say usually leaves an impression on people.					
3	I rarely have some nervous mannerisms in my speech.					
4	When I disagree with somebody I am very quick to challenge them.					
5	I can always repeat back to a person exactly what was meant.					
6	My eyes reflect exactly what I am feeling when I communicate.					

7	I dramatize a lot.					
8	Usually I tell people much about myself even before I get to know them well.					
9	In most social situations I generally speak very frequently.					
10	I am a very precise communicator.					
11	To be friendly, I habitually acknowledge verbally other's contributions.					
12	I leave people with an impression of me which they definitely tend to remember.					
13	I am a very relaxed communicator.					
14	I am very argumentative.					
15	Usually, I deliberately react in such a way that people know that I am listening to them.					

16	I tend to constantly gesture when I communicate.					
17	Regularly I tell jokes, anecdotes and stories when I communicate.					
18	I am an extremely open communicator.					
19	I am dominant in social situations.					
20	In arguments I insist upon very precise definitions.					
21	I am always an extremely friendly communicator.					
22	I leave a definite impression on people.					
23	The rhythm or flow of my speech is rarely affected by my nervousness.					
24	Once I get wound up in a heated discussion I have a hard time stopping myself.					

25	I really like to listen very carefully to people.					
26	I am very expressive nonverbally in social situations.					
27	Often I physically and vocally act out what I want to communicate.					
28	I readily reveal personal things about myself.					
29	I try to take charge of things when I am with people.					
30	I like to be strictly accurate when I communicate.					
31	Whenever I communicate, I tend to be very encouraging to people.					
32	The way I say something usually leaves an impression on people					
33	Under pressure I come across as a relaxed speaker.					

34	It bothers me to drop an argument that is not resolved.					
35	I am an extremely attentive communicator.					
36	I actively use a lot of facial expressions when I communicate.					
37	I very frequently verbally exaggerate to emphasize a point.					
38	As a rule, I openly express my feelings and emotions.					
39	In most social situations I tend to come on strong.					
40	Very often I insist that other people document or present some kind of proof for what they are arguing.					

Score:

This questionnaire taps into the ten basic dimensions of communication style:

Friendly (1, 11, 21, 31)
Impression leaving (2, 12, 22, 32)
Relaxed (3, 13, 23, 33)

Contentious (4, 14, 24, 34)
Attentive (5, 15, 25, 35)
Animated (6, 16, 26, 36)
Dramatic (7, 17, 27, 37)
Open (8, 18, 28, 38)
Dominant (9, 19, 29, 39)
Precise (10, 20, 30, 40)

Score your response to each question as follows:

"Strongly Disagree" = 1
"Disagree" = 2
"Neutral" = 3
"Agree" = 4
"Strongly Agree" = 5

Your score on each dimension will range from 4 to 20. The higher your score for any dimension, the more that dimension characterizes your communication style.

Interpretation:

The ten basic dimensions of face-to-face communication are:

- **Friendly**: confirms, strokes, and positively recognizes others.

- **Impression leaving**: being remembered because of the communicative stimuli that you project.

- **Relaxed**: reflects calmness, peace, and serenity and on the other hand, it suggests confidence and comfortableness.
- **Contentious**: argumentative.

- **Attentive**: responsive and showing feedback.

- **Animated**: uses frequent and sustained eye contact, many facial expressions, and gestures often.

- **Dramatic**: manipulates and exaggerates stories and uses other stylistic devices to highlight content.

- **Open**: being conversational, expansive, affable, convivial, gregarious, unreserved, somewhat frank, definitely extroverted, and obviously approachable.

- **Dominant**: tends to dominate and take charge of social interactions.

- **Precise**: seeks accurate and correct information.

When you review your results, consider to what degree your scores aid or hinder your communication effectiveness. High scores for being attentive and open would almost always be positive qualities. A high score for contentious, on the other hand, could be a negative in some situations. In addition, your scores might offer guidance in choosing a career. For instance, a high score on friendliness would likely be a good match for customer-service jobs, while a high score on contentiousness might be a valuable asset for a trial lawyer.

How Good Am I At Problem Solving?

Instructions:

For each of the below statements, rate how true it is for you using the following four-point scale. Try to respond as honestly as you can and work quickly:

		Never True For Me	Occasionally True For Me	Often True For Me	Always True For Me
1	I usually try to be clear about what is required from a task				
2	I know what needs to be done first and what can be left until later				
3	I ask myself lots of different questions about the nature of the problem				
4	I set myself targets rather than trying to do everything at once				
5	I usually avoid jumping at the first solution to a problem I come up with				
6	I can usually see more than one possible solution to a problem				

7	I listen to other people's suggestions and take note of them				
8	I do careful research to find a solution that will work				
9	I can weigh up different options to find the best solution to a problem				
10	I try to address the political issues and other consequences of the change I'm proposing so that others will understand and support my solution				
11	I evaluate potential solutions carefully and thoroughly against clear and consistent criteria				
12	I stay calm when I have to make an important decision				
13	Once I choose a solution, I develop an implementation plan with the sequence of events necessary for completion				
14	I can track my progress through a task by comparing my performance with my goals				
15	I can usually work out resources needs to solve problems				

16	I am comfortable working within constraints and limits, such as a deadlines and budget				
17	I think about how I will know it when a problem has been solved				
18	If my solution doesn't work, I work out why				
19	After a solution has been implemented, I look for ways to improve the idea and avoid future problem				
20	I find it important to look at the process of problem solving, not just the results				

Score:

This questionnaire taps into the five steps of the problem solving process:

Defining the problem (items 1, 2, 3, and 4)
Generating alternative solutions (items 5, 6, 7, and 8)
Evaluating alternatives and making a decision (items 9, 10, 11, and 12)
Implementing the selected solution (items 13, 14, 15, and 16)
Evaluating the results (items 17, 18, 19, and 20)

Score your response to each question as follows:

"Never True For Me" = 1
"Occasionally True For Me" = 2

"Often True For Me" = 3
"Always True For Me" = 4

Your score on each step of the problem solving process will vary between 4 and 16. The higher a step score, the better you perform at that step. Your overall score will fall between 20 and 80:

60-80 = confident problem solver
40-60 = average problem solver
20-40 = needs development

Interpretation:

Problem solving skills are needed in virtually every job and in everyday life. It's important then that you understand and effectively follow the steps of the problem solving process to resolve problems you might face in your work, education, or personal life. The five steps of the problem solving process are:

- **Defining the problem**: information is gathered, processing, and deliberated. It is important to clarify goals for solving the problem by identifying exactly what a solution should accomplish.

- **Generating alternative solutions**: identifying viable alternatives that could resolve the problem.

- **Evaluating alternatives and making a decision**: more information is gathered, data are analyzed, and the advantages and disadvantages for every possible alternative course of action are identified. A decision is then made by selecting the preferred alternative.

- **Implementing the selected solution**: involves taking actions to make sure the solution decided upon becomes a reality.

- Evaluating the results: comparing the actual and desired results to insure that the problem has really been solved or that no undesired side effects have occurred. Both positive and negative consequences of the chosen solution should be examined. If the problem hasn't been solved, you need to repeat the earlier steps.

How Good Am I At Time Management?

<u>Instructions:</u>

Complete the following questionnaire by selecting Yes or No for each item. Force yourself to respond Yes or No. Be frank and allow your responses to create an accurate picture of how you tend to respond to this kind of situations.

		Yes	No
1	When confronted with several items of similar urgency and importance. I tend to do the easiest one first.		
2	I do the most important things during that part of the day when I know I perform best.		
3	Most of the time I don't do things someone else can do; I delegate this type of work to others.		
4	Even though meeting without a clear and useful purpose upset me, I put up with them.		
5	I skim documents before reading them and don't complete any that offer a low value.		
6	I don't worry much if I don't accomplish at least one significant task each day.		
7	I save the most trivial tasks for that time of day when my creative energy is lowest.		

8	My workspace is neat and organized.		
9	My office door is always "open"; I never work in complete privacy.		
10	I schedule my time completely from start to finish every workday.		
11	I don't like "to do" lists, preferring to respond to daily events as they occur.		
12	I "block" a certain amount of time each day or week that is dedicated to high-priority activities.		

Score:

Calculate your score based on the number of "Yes" answers to items 2, 3, 5, 7, 8, and 12. If you answered "Yes" to those you received one point for each. If you answered "No" to items 1, 4, 6, 9, 10, and 11 then you received a point for each. Add the "Yes" points and the "No" points together.

Interpretation:

The higher the total score, the better your time management skills. Reread those items where your responses did not match the recommended one in the "Score" section. Why don't they match? Do you have reasons why your behavior in this instance should be different from the recommended guidelines? Think about what you can do (and how easily it can be done) to adjust your behavior to be more consistent with these recommendations.

Do I Have What It Takes To Become An Entrepreneur?

Instructions:

Select your most appropriate answer for the following questions:

1. What portion of your college expenses did you earn (or are you earning)?
a)   50 percent or more
b)   Less than 50 percent
c)   None

2. In college, your academic performance was/is:
a)   Above average
b)   Average
c)   Below average

3. What is your basic reason for considering opening a business?
a)   I want to make money.
b)   I want to control my own destiny.
c)   I hate the frustration of working for someone else.

4. Which phrase best describes your attitude toward work?
a)   I can keep going as long as I need to; I don't mind working for something I want.
b)   I can work hard for a while, but when I've had enough, I quit.
c)   Hard work really doesn't get you anywhere.

5. How would you rate your organizational skills?
a)   Super organized
b)   Above average
c)   Average
d)   I do well to find half the things I look for.

6. You are primarily a(n):

a) optimist

b) Pessimist

c) Neither

7. You are faced with a challenging problem. As you work, you realize you are stuck. You will most likely:

a) Give up

b) Ask for help

c) Keep plugging: you'll figure it out

8. You are playing a game with a group of friends. You are most interested in:

a) Winning

b) Playing well

c) Making sure everyone has a good time

d) cheating as much as possible

9. How would you describe your feelings toward failure?

a) Fear of failure paralyzes me.

b) Failure can be a good learning experience.

c) Knowing that I might fail motivates me to work even harder.

d) "Damn the torpedoes! Full speed ahead."

10. Which phrase best describes you?

a) I need constant encouragement to get anything done.

b) If someone gets me started, I can keep going.

c) I am energetic and hard-working -- a self-starter.

11. Which bet would you most likely accept (If we assume betting is not forbidden by your religion)?

a) A wager on a dog race

b) A wager on a racquetball game in which you play an opponent

c) Neither. I never make wagers.

12. At the horse derby, you would bet on (If we assume betting is not forbidden by your religion):

a)   The 100-to-1 long shot
b)   The odds-on favorite
c)   The 3-to-1 shot
d)   None of the above

Score:

You will be given 10 points for each of the following answers: 1a, 2a, 3c, 4a, 5a, 6a, 7c, 8a, 9c, 10c, 11b, and 12c.

You will be given 8 points for each of the following answers: 3b, 8b, and 9b.

You will be given 6 points for 2b and 5b.

You will be given 5 points for lb.

You will be given 4 points for 5c.

Toy will be given 2 points for: 2c, 3a, 4b, 6c, 9d, 10b, 11a, and 12b.

Any other answered will be given 0 points.

Interpretation:

This assessment offers an impression of your likelihood to become a successful entrepreneur. It compares your characteristics with those of typical entrepreneurs. You may locate your Entrepreneurship Profile (EP) score as follows.

100 + = Entrepreneur extraordinaire
80-99 = Entrepreneur
60-79 = Potential entrepreneur
0-59 = Entrepreneur in the rough

What's My Tendency To Suffer Stress?

Instructions:

Complete the following questionnaire. Select the number that best represents your tendency to behave on each bipolar dimension.

	1	2	3	4	5	6	7	8	
Am casual about appointments									Am never late
Am not competitive									Am very competitive
Never feel rushed									always feel rushed
Take things one at a time									Try to do many things at once
Do things slowly									Do things fast
Express feelings									"Sit on feelings"
Have many interests									Have few interests but work

Score:

Sum the numbers for all items and then multiply that sum by three to give you a total score. Scores of 100 and above are considered Type A; scores under 100 are considered Type B.

Interpretation:

Type A personality describes someone who is aggressively involved in a chronic, incessant struggle to achieve more and more in less and less time. More specifically, Type As are always moving, walking, and eating rapidly; feel impatient with the pace of most events; strive to do two or more things at once; do not cope well with leisure time; and are obsessed with numbers, measuring their success in terms of how many or how much of everything they acquire. Type A's can be difficult to get along with because they are so driven. They're not particularly good team players. In contrast, Type B's are the exact opposites.

If you score in the "A" categories, you need to be aware of your tendency to focus on quantity over quality. You may do better in jobs that are routine and rely on speed rather than creativity for success. You are also probably better matched to jobs where you can work alone rather than on teams. And recognize that you may become frustrated working on long-term projects because of your need to see results. Finally, Type As often experience moderate to high levels of stress. So if you're type A, identify stress-management techniques that work for you and use them.

Appendix (B): Career Plan Template

ADMINISTRATIVE INFORMATION

Name: _____

Frequency of Review: _____

Period Covered: From _____ To _____

Next Review Date: _____

MY CAREER PROFILE

My Interests (top 3 themes in your self-assessment "What Are My Career Interests?"):

My Motivators (top 3 skills in your self-assessment "What Motivates Me At Work?"):

My Skills (top 3 motivators in your self-assessment "What Are My Skills?"):

MY CAREER OPTIONS

	Comments (e.g., prerequisites, requirements, obstacles, etc.)	Desired Lifestyle Supported? (Y/N)
Option 1: _____	_____ _____ _____	_____
Option 2: _____	_____ _____ _____	_____
Option 3: _____	_____ _____ _____	_____

MY CAREER GOALS

	Goal	How Does It Support My Career Choice?	Skills I Must Acquire To Reach That Goal	How Will I Acquire These Skills?	Resources I Need (Money, Staff, etc.)	People Who Will Support Me	Time Frame
Short-range (1 Year)							
Mid-range (2 Years)							
Long-range (3-5 Years)							

174

MY CAREER RISK MANAGEMENT PLAN

Risk	Risk Rating (H/M/L)	Career Goals Impacted	Counteracting Measures

Appendix (C): Useful Websites

	Website	What For?
1	www.onetonline.org	Primary occupational database with skills, abilities, knowledge, and work environment profiles for all jobs in the sixteen defined career clusters.
2	www.careertech.org	Information on certificates and licenses required for all jobs in the sixteen defined career clusters.
3	www.internships.com	Internship listings, software and reports for students, educators and employers. The largest database devoted to internships in the world.
4	www.resumetemplates.com	Resume writing as an MS Word or PDF document. Choice of professional templates. Packed full of samples, phrases, and action words to use.
5	www.visualcv.com	Online resume builder with tools for creating multimedia resumes that incorporate video, images, charts and audio.
6	www.salaryexpert.com	Access to updated salary rates for over 100,000 job titles in 69 countries, and cost of living information.
7	www.indeed.com	Search engine for jobs that gives job seekers free access to millions of employment opportunities from thousands of websites.

8	www.monster.com	Top recruitment website that offers Job search, resume management, career advice, and chats and message boards on various topics.
9	www.careerbuilder.com	Top recruitment website that offers Job search, resume posting and career advice.
10	www.simplyhired.com	Top recruitment website that offers Job search and resume posting.